PERFECT PHRASES™

for

ESL

Everyday Situations

**Hundreds of Ready-to-Use Phrases That Help
You Navigate Any English-Language Situation
in Your Daily Life**

Natalie Gast

Mc
Graw
Hill

New York   Chicago   San Francisco   Lisbon   London   Madrid   Mexico City
Milan   New Delhi   San Juan   Seoul   Singapore   Sydney   Toronto

Also by Natalie Gast:
Perfect Phrases for ESL: Everyday Business Life
Perfect Phrases for ESL: Advancing Your Career

Contents

Part 2   Health and Medical Situations

Preface

As an instructor and trainer to non-native English speakers, I have always understood the difficulties my English as a Second Language (ESL) students face. Adjusting to change—a new country, a different culture, a foreign language, a new career—is challenging and may create a crisis. In December 2010, I actually became one of you. **I walked in your shoes**.

I moved my home and my work from New Jersey to Hollywood, Florida, both in the United States. Moving—packing, unpacking, and discarding meaningful items and memories—was difficult, but I knew it would be. What I didn't realize was that moving within the United States, on the same coast, only two and a half hours away by plane, where the same language is spoken and the same career exists, would present so many situations in which I would feel **frustrated**, **inadequate**, and **bewildered**. I **felt like a fish out of water**. I often had the **urge** to **withdraw**.

Problem situations **ranged from** the **silly** to the serious. They included finding a good place to get a haircut, registering to vote, and researching doctors and hospitals in a new location. Learning rules and regulations of new living quarters, researching public transportation, and investigating employment opportunities became everyday activities.

Change can be **risky**, but it also presents opportunities. Change may be the opportunity to grow emotionally, linguistically, and in many other ways. What I have done—and urge you do—is **push through** the feelings of discomfort instead of **isolating** myself and withdrawing. Take chances in your new environment and with your new language. Become an active language learner. Follow the ideas for active learning at the start of each part of this book and any other **techniques** you **come up with**. Don't be afraid to **think outside the box**. Happy learning!

Who Can Benefit from Using This Book

You can and will benefit from using *Perfect Phrases for ESL: Everyday Situations* if you are an adult learner of the American English language, whether you are learning English as a Second Language (ESL), English for Speakers of Other Languages (ESOL), or English as a Foreign Language (EFL). English learners, who are about to travel to the United States or have recently arrived, especially may benefit from phrases offered in the text because of the new situations with which they will likely have to **cope**.

In the chapters of Part 1, this book offers attention to the educational system in the United States, including choices for you to investigate for your children and yourself. There are numerous phrases you may hear during your search for learning opportunities. Additionally, there are phrases for you to say that will **aid** you when you call, visit, or inquire about these locations. The word choices present you with new vocabulary and idioms as well as sentences in which you can **plug in** your own specific thoughts.

Part 2 provides phrases to use when inquiring about medically related situations such as visits to the doctor, dentist, hospital, and pharmacy.

Community resources are **addressed** as well. The chapters in Part 3 offer phrases for getting services from the bank, the library, and the post office, as well as information and emergency help from the fire and police departments. Phrases to use when shopping for food, putting gas in your car, and finding auto repair help are included in Part 4, "Around Town."

There are Active Language Advice activities at the start of each part as well as in the appendix. Learning a language, as we know, is a life's work, and serious language learners are always open to additional **techniques** for doing this work. There are also sections that pay attention to situations the higher-level learner may not have encountered yet in the United States, such as hiring a nanny or reporting an emergency.

How to Use This Book

Perfect Phrases for ESL: Everyday Situations, like most other books, may be read from beginning to end, and if you have the time, that is a good way to read it. If you are an EFL (English as a Foreign Language) student studying English in a non-English-speaking country and preparing to travel to the United States, that would be a particularly good way to go through this book. It gives you some background information on education, medical, and community service issues in the United States either before or soon after you arrive, as well as vocabulary and idiomatic expressions you may not have studied in your EFL classes.

To quote the words of a Toastmasters local club past president, who lived and worked in several countries and taught himself several languages while abroad, "The way to gain an **intimate** knowledge of a language is to learn its idioms and learn about its country's culture."

This text also gives you the phrases for many situations you may encounter immediately upon arriving in the United States. Therefore, for high beginner and intermediate ESL or ESOL learners who have been living in the United States, a more as-needed approach also could work. For example, if you have been in the United States for some time and need a dental appointment, you could turn to Chapter 6 before making the call. It would, however, be a good idea to read Chapter 9, "First Responders," to learn phrases to use in an emergency before you may need that information. If you do that, you will be prepared, just **in case**.

Those who have read my previously published ESL books in McGraw-Hill's *Perfect Phrases* series—*Perfect Phrases for ESL: Everyday Business Life* and *Perfect Phrases for ESL: Advancing Your Career*—may also wish to look at this *Perfect Phrases* book. They may find vocabulary, idioms, and phrases that were not in the prior publications because the subject matter in this book is survival-related, rather than work-related as in the prior texts.

Readers have commented that the size (dimensions) and weight of the books in this series are real **advantages**; the books may easily be taken in a purse or a **handbag**, a briefcase or an attaché case, or even a beach bag. They may also be put into the glove compartment of your car to be read while waiting to pick up the children at school, a friend at a bus or train station, or visitors at an airport. The books are also a good size to **leaf through** if you are having a meal alone at a restaurant.

Remember to use this book as it best **suits** your learning style. Write notes on the blank pages at the ends of each part, underline or highlight words or phrases you want to remember, **dog-ear** pages, or attach **Post-it Notes** to pages. Add your own words or phrases to what is printed in the book.

The *Perfect Phrases for ESL* series lends itself to study group or classroom use as well. Have fun, and learn from the books and from each other.

Idioms and Other Vocabulary

Addressed: paid attention to

Advantages: good qualities, useful benefits

Aid: help make a situation easier

Bewildered: confused

Come up with: think of, think what will help you

Cope: handle, deal with

Dog-ear: turn down the corner of a page to mark a place in a book

Felt like a fish out of water: felt as if in totally unfamiliar surroundings

Frustrated: upset because one cannot control a situation

In case: in the event that

Inadequate: not up to handling a situation

Intimate knowledge: detailed knowledge

Isolating: separating yourself from other people

Leaf through: turn the pages of a book or magazine

Plug in: insert, add, put in

Post-it Notes: the trademark name for a small piece of sticky paper, used for notes

Push through: get past without giving up

Ranged from: include from one thing to another and everything between

Risky: has a possibility of something bad happening

Silly: not serious

Suits: fits in with

Techniques: special ways to do something

Think outside the box: think of unusual ways to do something.

Urge: strong wish

Walked in your shoes: understood what you have gone through by going through the same situation

Withdraw: separate from a situation, pull back from, stop participating

Acknowledgments

To all my students who have, over the years, asked many of the probing questions that appear on these pages, and to all my colleagues who have helped me to answer these questions. Thank you.

To my son, Andrew Gast, my daughter-in-law, Jodi Gast, and my grandsons, Leo and Nico, for giving me reasons to move to southeast Florida. Thank you.

To my son, Eric Gast, my niece, Linda Diamond, and my former office manager, Gail Gallagher, who have dragged reluctant me into the computer age. Thanks for being patient and encouraging.

To Harriet Diamond, my sister, Walter Ladden, and Andi Jeszenszky, all three always there. Also to Nancy Barr, newly there. Thanks for your much-appreciated efforts.

To Holly McGuire, my very talented and supportive editor at McGraw-Hill, and Grace Freedson, my agent, for introducing me to Holly and McGraw-Hill. Thanks to you both, again, for the opportunity.

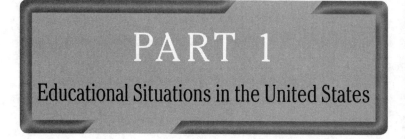

PART 1

Educational Situations in the United States

Active Learning Advice: Don't Wait to Use Your English!

Don't wait for that special future time when you **expect** to be able to communicate in English error free. Unless you practice, that moment will never come. Take your English language skills, **though limited**, and use them. Begin every **encounter** with "Hello," "Hi," "Nice to meet you," or "Glad to see you again." At each **parting** say, "Good-bye," "So long," "Hope to see you again," or "I'm sure we'll talk again soon."

Speak English to people in stores, in offices, and in schools.

Read English newspapers (if only the **captions** under the pictures), magazines, **junk mail**, **cartoons**, **the comics**, children's books (with or without children), and **"trashy" novels**. **Highlight** or **underline** words you don't understand, and look them up in your dictionary or on your computer.

Write **shopping lists**, **recipes**, and notes. Stick **Post-it Notes** on items you want to remember the English names for.

Listen to everything you hear in English—song **lyrics**, **talk radio**, voice mail messages, and whatever anyone says (unless it's private)—and ask questions. This may sound strange; aren't listening and hearing the same? No, they are not! If you are able to hear (are not **deaf**) and are within hearing distance of the sound, what's the problem? Hearing is **passive**, and listening is **active**; it's about **choosing** to **process** what you have heard.

Don't Forget Small Talk

"Small talk" is friendly conversation about unimportant subjects. We use small talk as a way to generate more conversation. It is an accepted and common way to begin the day, whether at work or during day-to-day errands.

Phrases for Small Talk

→ I'm cold; I can't wait until spring.

→ It looks like it's going to snow. I hope it won't be **deep**.

→ What did you watch on TV this weekend?

→ **Rush hour** was terrible this morning, wasn't it?

→ I like your coat. I need a new coat. Where did you buy that one?

→ I like green. Green is a good color on you.

→ Have you decided on a name for the baby yet?

→ How is your daughter feeling?

→ What are you having for lunch? I'm having **noodles**.

→ Please tell me more about **Valentine's Day**. There are so many **greeting cards** for it.

→ My **horoscope** says, "This is a **lucky** day for me." What about yours?

Idioms and Other Vocabulary

Active: doing something to make results happen

Captions: words printed under a picture in a newspaper or magazine to describe the picture

Cartoons: drawings, often funny, political, and with words

Choosing: deciding on something

Deaf: physically unable to hear

Deep: far down from a surface

Encounter: meet up with

Expect: think will happen

Greeting cards: cards to send for special reasons (birthday, anniversary, holidays such as Christmas), sympathy cards for sad occasions (death in a family), get-well cards (for a person with an illness)

Highlight: bring attention to by marking with a colored pen

Horoscope: prediction of what will happen to you based on the position of the stars and planets and the date of your birth

Junk mail: letters and other written material sent as advertisements (ads)

Limited: not big or of great size

Lucky: likely to experience good things

Lyrics: words of a song

Noodles: soft strips or shapes of food made from flour, water, and eggs

Parting: leaving, saying good-bye

Passive: accepting what happens without being actively involved in the situation

Post-it Notes: trademark name for small pieces of paper that stick and are used for notes

Process: be involved in

Recipes: directions or instructions for cooking

Rush hour: time when people travel to and from work and when there is increased traffic

Shopping lists: lists of things you need to buy at a store, mostly food items

Talk radio: radio programs in which people talk about news and opinions and sometimes listeners call into the radio station to talk

The comics: story told through a series of cartoons

Though (*also* **although** *or* **tho'** *or* **altho'**): relates two events that occur at the same time or almost at the same time, even if it is surprising that they do happen this way. (This happened altho' that happened.)

Trashy novels: bad-quality, but often entertaining, written fiction

Underline: put a line under to bring attention to

Valentine's Day: holiday on February 14 (2/14) when people give cards, candy, and other gifts to people they love (husband, wife, parents, children, and even sometimes teachers and friends)

CHAPTER 1

Babysitters, Nannies, Day Care, and Early Learning Centers

C hild care is an important concern for all parents, and there is more concern in a new country. This chapter offers perfect phrases related to child care.

Babysitters

Babysitting is a **term** used for taking care of young children while their parents are **occupied**. The services of a babysitter are usually for several hours at a time. Perhaps one parent is working while the other has an appointment, or a **couple** is going out for the evening. Daytime adult classes or meeting **venues** may offer babysitting services free or for a small fee to pay the babysitter. The good part of this **scenario** is that the babysitter has been selected and has **credentials** and/or training for the job.

If you need a babysitter and have to find one on your own, it is important to get referrals from neighbors, colleagues, a medical office, a school, or a hospital. Interview the babysitter before hiring her or him, and if you can, have a **dry run**: hire the potential babysitter for a short time, do something in another room, and observe the interaction between the babysitter and your child or children. You may want to observe interactions in several situations—playtime, mealtime, and bedtime.

Phrases to Use When Interviewing a Babysitter

→ Have you babysat before? How often?

→ How long have you been babysitting?

→ Have you taken a course in babysitting at your school or community center?

→ How many hours was the course?

→ Did you get a certificate for taking a course in babysitting, and may I see it?

→ How old are the children you have babysat for?

→ Have you babysat _____ (during the day when the children are awake, during the night after the children are asleep)?

→ What do you do when the children are sleeping?

→ What are your thoughts about **discipline**?

→ What are your feelings about the children watching TV or videos?

→ What children's _____ (TV shows, videos, games, books) are you familiar with?

→ Have you taken a course in _____ (**first aid**, mouth-to-mouth resuscitation, **CPR**)?

→ What has been _____ (the most difficult, unusual, funniest, **scariest**) babysitting experience you have had?

→ How much _____ (do you charge, do you make, do you make an hour)?

What You May and May Not Ask Job Applicants

Remember equal employment opportunity laws. When you interview a candidate for a babysitting or nanny position, as well as any job, there are federal laws that apply to asking questions to all job applicants. Allowable questions relate to their skills and experience. You may ask for references.

The areas you may not ask questions about include age, race, religion, place of birth, marital status, disabilities, and arrests. Many companies provide, at a cost, background checks, and you may choose to hire them to check criminal, driving, and financial records.

There are good questions to ask the references that your applicant has given you at your request. These include:

What are his/her strengths and weaknesses?

Is he/she reliable?

Why did the previous employment end, and would you rehire him/her?

Are there concerns about the number of children he/she would be responsible for or concerns about the ages of the children he/she would be in charge of?

How does he/she handle stress and **multitasking**?

Does he/she have special **position-related** skills?

The best way to hire for these positions is always a recommendation from someone who has used the babysitter or the nanny.

Phrases for Instructing the Babysitter

→ I/We use _____ (**time-out**, no dessert, no **play date**) as a punishment.

→ I/We take away TV if the children misbehave.

→ Let us know if the children _____ (**act up**, misbehave).

→ I/We never spank the children.

→ I/We never send the children to bed without dinner.

→ I/We would like you to be involved with the children when they are awake.

→ They like to read one book before bedtime.

→ I/We want you to _____ (play games, read stories, help with homework) with them.

→ I/We don't want _____ (**playing rough**, using the swimming pool, driving with the children in the car).

→ I/We don't want you to have _____ (visitors, long phone conversations, computer time) during work.

→ If the baby cries, pick him/her up.

→ Have you ever put children to bed?

➜ We put the baby in her crib at 7:30.

➜ Have you fed the children yet?

➜ The kids should eat everything on their plates.

➜ Don't worry if the kids don't eat everything.

➜ _____ (child's name) is a picky eater.

➜ They are not allowed dessert unless they eat their vegetables.

➜ Have you ever changed diapers?

➜ Put dirty diapers in this hamper.

➜ Have you given children a bath?

➜ Make sure they brush their teeth.

➜ _____ (child's name) likes a night-light in his room at bedtime.

➜ _____ (child's name) likes this blanket.

➜ Call us if you have any problems.

➜ Here is our cell phone number.

➜ We can be reached at _____ (this restaurant, the Smiths' home, the kids' school). Here are the telephone numbers.

Idioms and Other Vocabulary

Act up: behave badly

Couple: two (a couple of books), two people in a romantic relationship, a husband and wife

CPR: cardiopulmonary resuscitation, breathing in someone's mouth and pressing on his or her chest to restart breathing and the heart beating

Credentials: documents that show you are able to perform in a position

Discipline: training used to change negative behavior into positive behavior by giving consequences for negative behavior

Dry run: practice session for the actual event

First aid: basic medical attention given quickly

Multitasking: doing two or more things at the same time.

Occupied: busy, doing something

Play date: appointment for children to play with each other

Playing rough: playing in a way in which someone might get injured

Position-related: having to do with one's job or work

Scariest: making you feel the most afraid, frightened, scared

Scenario: situation that may occur

Spank: hit a child on the rear or backside as a form of punishment

Term: word

Time-out: in sports, time taken from a game to rethink how to continue the game; in child care, a punishment in which children must stop playing and be alone to rethink their actions

Venues: places where activities happen

Nannies

A nanny takes care of a child or children for a family in the family's home and for a longer time and much more regularly than a babysitter. The nanny may be paid by the hour, but more often by the day, week, or longer period. It is a regular employment situation, so **references** and **background checks** should be

verified carefully. Often benefits come with the nanny position. A common benefit is **paid vacation** time, which is time away from work while receiving pay equal to your salary for the same period of time.

A nanny may take care of one or more children for working parents or for a single working parent full-time. The nanny often acts as a part of the family. Nannies are most often women; there are, however, male nannies. Families that employ a male nanny sometimes say that they appreciate having a positive **male influence** from someone who serves as a **role model**, especially for sons.

Phrases for interviewing nannies include many or most of those used for interviewing babysitters, but there are additional phrases. When you are interviewing and hiring a nanny, it is, of course, really an advantage to **hit the ground running**. Get a **head start** by checking out recommended candidates with neighbors, colleagues, the human resources (**HR**) department where you or your spouse work, or even an agency. You still have to conduct serious interviewing, but some questions may already be answered.

Phrases to Say When Interviewing a Nanny

→ Where did you _____ (study, learn, get a license, get certified) to become a nanny?

→ Did you _____ (study, learn, earn a certificate, get a license) to become a nanny, and may I see your credentials?

→ Would this be your first position as a nanny? What type of work did you do before this?

→ Have you worked as a nanny before? Where? Do you have references?

→ How many children were in the family or families you worked with?

→ Why did you leave your last position?

→ Did you live in the home of the family?

→ Did you **commute**?

→ How many _____ (hours, days) did you work during a week?

→ What were the _____ (time off, vacation time) arrangements?

→ Can you _____ (cook, drive, speak [your language], perform CPR, mouth-to-mouth resuscitation, first aid)?

→ Do you have a certificate in _____ (first aid, swimming, lifesaving, CPR)?

→ We don't allow _____ (smoking, drinking) in front of our children.

→ Do you go to bed early or very late?

→ What _____ (music, TV programs) do you like to _____ (listen to, watch)?

→ Do you like to watch or participate in sports?

→ Are you a U.S. citizen?

→ Do you have a visitor's visa? Do you have a green card?

→ Do you drive? Do you own a car?

→ What are your thoughts on discipline?

e in the moment, so it isn't appropriate

scipline until the child returns home. Many

_____ (time-out, removal of privileges,

tely with the child about the **incident**) at

ounselor will discuss our discipline policy and

work together.

ay When Visiting an Early
nter or Preschool

our **accreditation documents**?

ern is my child's **safety** and **security**.

nter's _____ (**philosophy of learning**,

licy, **attitude** about teaching or **modeling**

tio of adults to children _____ (in a

ts, for one-year-olds, with four-year-olds)?

iscipline young children?

andle the _____ (eating, napping,

er) scheduling?

bus or van, and how long has he or she

or you? What is the driver's safety record?

center **celebrate** _____ (**diverse**

nt languages, **holidays**)?

_____ (training, special training, developmen-

going preparation) do the _____

s, assistants, other staff members)

ave, get, receive)?

→ How do you handle a child who refuses to _____ (eat, go to bed, wash his or her hands before a meal, share with a brother or sister)?

→ What do you do with a child who won't stop _____ (crying, biting another child, screaming in a store for toys or candy)?

→ When the children are _____ (sleeping, napping, in school, at music lessons), what are your feelings about _____ (cooking, cleaning, ironing, doing the wash, shopping for food, performing other household duties)?

→ We _____ (return to [your country], take a vacation) every _____ (summer, Christmas, month) and would like you to have the same time for your _____ (vacation, paid vacation).

→ We would like the house _____ (closed, rented, occupied by our friends) then, so do you have a place to live?

Idioms and Other Vocabulary

Background checks: verification that what someone has told you about his or her past education, employment, etc., is true

Commute: travel back and forth between work and your home

Head start: a lead, an advantage

Hit the ground running: have a head start to be successful at what you are doing

HR: human resources department (Many people just pronounce the initials.)

Male influence: a man's effect on, example of behavior

References: letters from people for whom you have worked, people who know you from your educational background, and people who know you from your past and can offer personal references, which say nice things about your character qualities such as honesty

Role model: someone you admire and want to pattern your behavior after

Verified: checked out

Day Care

The first step in the public school system in the United States is **kindergarten**. The age at which children in the United States begin kindergarten is usually five. However, many parents choose earlier education opportunities. These choices may be called day care, early learning centers, preschool, or nursery school. Day care and early learning centers are often for infants up to kindergarten age. The other options—nursery school and preschool—may take children from two or three years old to when they start kindergarten in the public school system.

Early learning centers or day care facilities are locations at which you **drop off** children or send them, if they are old enough, by bus or van for a number of days during the week. Children are cared for and involved in learning and play that challenges their minds and bodies for as many hours during a day as needed. The need depends on a parent's work schedule and feelings about having the child **exposed to** other children, teachers, and activities.

Before you decide on a place that is **appropriate** for your child, visit several centers. Take a complete tour of the facilities, observe the teachers and the students, and ask questions. You will be

turning your child over t(
to make them *not* be com
check—a thorough inspe
general environment (D(
clean, or does it smell like
a lot of garbage and tras
dren and the teachers (A
who will meet your chil(
child is being driven to t

Phrases You Ma
Center or Presc

→ Our center serves

→ Our center offers
early learning.

→ Our teachers and
the best experien

→ We work with pa
pline matters.

→ We have many a
participation an

→ We like the chil(
children, to brin
time. A **teddy l**
children to brin
make the **trans**
the children.

→ **Children liv**
to wait to di
parents use
talking priva
home. Our **c**
how we can

Phrases to :
Learning Ce

→ May I check y

→ My main conc

→ What is the ce
discipline po
social skills)?

→ What is the **ra**
class, for infan

→ How do you d

→ How do you **h**
playing togeth

→ Who drives th
been driving f

→ How does the
cultures, differ

→ What _____
tal activities, o
(teachers, **aide**
_____ (

Phrases About Activities and Learning

→ What will my child be doing all day, and why?

→ What are the activities for _____ (my child's age group, infants, one-year-olds, four-year-olds)?

→ How are the children learning? What are the **materials** and **methods**, and what are the reasons for using these?

→ What _____ (learning games, language activities, physical play) do the two- and three-year-olds participate in?

→ I _____ (understand, have read, have heard) that **finger painting strengthens** hands and fingers and is a **lead-in** to **handwriting**. When are children exposed to finger painting?

→ Do the teachers have _____ (different cultural backgrounds, dual-language ability, multi-language skills)?

Phrases About Special Needs

→ I am new to the United States.

→ I just started learning English.

→ We speak _____ (your language) at home.

→ How can I help my child with homework when I don't speak English?

→ Do you _____ (give, require) homework for the four- to five-year-olds?

→ Are you able to **recommend** _____ (a **tutor**, a way for my child and me to learn English together)?

→ Are all of the teachers fluent in English? Are some of them bilingual or multilingual?

→ Does the center accept children with _____ (**physical disabilities**, learning issues, **special needs**)?

→ Do you conduct some activities in English and _____ (my language) as a bridge to learning English?

→ Does the center offer _____ (**testing**, **counseling**)?

Phrases for the First Day

→ I have brought a _____ (teddy bear, toy, family photo) for my child.

→ May I stay for a short time until my child _____ (stops crying, is more comfortable, becomes more relaxed)?

→ If I can't _____ (be here, sit with my child, wait for him or her to calm down), who will _____ (calm him or her down, control him or her, take care of him or her)?

→ What do you want me to do?

Idioms and Other Vocabulary

Accreditation documents: documents showing that schools have met required standards and gotten official approval

Aides: helpers

Appropriate: good, a good fit for

Attitude: opinion about a subject

Body language: movements of parts of your body that show what you are thinking without you speaking

Celebrate: treat as special

Children live in the moment: children only think about what is happening now as far as rewards and punishments

Counseling: emotionally supporting the children who attend the center and their parents

Counselor: a person whose job is counseling

Discipline policy: the center's official opinion about discipline at the center

Diverse: many different

Drop off: leave your child at the center after taking him or her to the destination

Exposed to: not protected from

Finger painting: painting with special paint and using fingers not brushes (Children do this activity.)

Handle: take care of

Handwriting: connected script writing

Holidays: days that celebrate historic or religious events

Incident: something that happens

Kindergarten: the first year in the public school system, which prepares children for first grade (Children start kindergarten at age five or six depending on their birth date.)

Lead into: prepare for

Materials: teaching tools used for learning, making, or doing something

Methods: ways of doing something

Modeling: showing good behavior you want to copy

Naptime: time devoted to a short sleep, called a nap (Young children nap during a long school day.)

On the same page: thinking in the same way as someone else about doing something

Philosophy of learning: ideas about learning

Physical disabilities: conditions that keep someone from doing all that others can do

Ratio: a relationship between two numbers or amounts

Recommend: make a suggestion after careful consideration

Safe: not dangerous

Safety: conditions without danger

Secure: protected

Security: protection

Sensory check: process of noticing everything that has to do with the five senses—sight, hearing, smell, taste, and touch

Social skills: ability to get along with people, good manners

Special needs: needs related to physical and/or mental problems

Strangers (*also* **total strangers**): people you don't know

Strengthens: makes strong

Teddy bear: a soft toy in the shape of a bear

Testing: a full range of evaluations

Transition: movement or change

Transitional: changing from one place to another, such as from home to day care

Tutor: someone who teaches one or a few students privately

Welcoming: designed to make people feel comfortable

CHAPTER 2

Elementary and High School

The early learning centers or nursery schools take your child up to five years old. At the age of five, depending on the month of their birth and the **cutoff date** in the school, children begin **mandatory** elementary school in kindergarten. Children who have not attended any of the preschool **options** begin kindergarten at this age as well. Some elementary or primary schools include kindergarten and continue through eighth grade; others continue only through fifth grade, and children then go on to junior high school or middle school for grades six, seven, and eight.

High school for all usually **comprises** grades nine, ten, eleven, and twelve. Ninth grade is called the freshman year of high school, tenth grade is the sophomore year, eleventh grade is the junior year, and twelfth grade is the senior year of high school in the public school system. A child is permitted to quit school legally at age sixteen, but this is **discouraged**. Those who do leave before finishing high school are called **dropouts**. A high school diploma is a definite **plus** in finding work, so dropouts often go on to earn a **GED**. Additionally, students who choose to attend a college in the United States must have completed coursework that is **equivalent to** what is taught in American high schools.

To register your child in public school, which is free for all residents of school age, you need to identify your school district and then your local school according to where you live within your town or city. Using the Internet, telephone, or in person, communicate with the board of education, go to the town or city hall, or just visit the principal's office of the school nearest your home. Sometimes parents **reverse** the process. If they have a preference for a particular school or school district, they try to buy or rent their living accommodations within the area served by that district. For doing that, a real estate agent could be helpful.

This may be a good time to visit your local library for information and direction. Librarians can be very helpful with information about the schools and may even cut through some **red tape**. When you visit the school, you will need to show a proof of residency (for example, a telephone bill, electric bill, water bill, lease, mortgage, or driver's license) with your name and local address on it. You will be asked for your child's medical files with a record of medical exams and vaccinations. The school will provide a medical form for your doctor to fill out.

Once registered, your child is eligible for many types of support to help him or her succeed in school. An **ESL** or **ESOL** instructor will help the student make the transition to an English-only classroom. Depending on the school, the student may be **mainstreamed** and take **pull-out classes** in English with other ESL students or be taught in a bilingual setting. In any case, help from a private tutor may be necessary at first. If the student has any disabilities (learning, **psychosocial**, **speech**, **reading**) that might interfere with learning, he or she may be eligible for services, free of charge and usually during school hours, from a specialist.

It really doesn't matter whether you are enrolling a child in kindergarten, the early grades, or especially high school; in every case, the transition is difficult for the student and for you. To manage the transition, you can gain an advantage by forming relationships with the people who know the school, the system, and **shortcuts** to reduce some of the stress.

Some people at the school you and your child should meet as soon as possible are the principal, the school secretary in the principal's office, your child's teachers, and any teaching aides in the classroom. Your child may also have additional teachers for special subjects such as gym or P.E. (physical education), music (vocal and/or instrumental), art, and others. You should also meet with the school **counselor**.

It is your responsibility to have school records, test results, and notes on your children translated into English. Your children may be tested and observed to determine the most appropriate placement. You will have a say in the placement process.

Phrases for Learning About Your New School

→ May I schedule an appointment to discuss my child's needs?

→ May I observe a class?

→ How do you address different learning styles?

➔ My child _____ (is a visual learner, learns best by listening, tends to move around a lot, likes to be active, is a hands-on learner, is extremely **shy** and afraid of speaking).

➔ Do you use computers in the classroom?

➔ Do we need a computer at home for homework? Can you suggest one that works for most of the students?

➔ Is there homework every night?

➔ Is there a list of school supplies my child should bring to school?

➔ At what grade do the students **change classes**, and how does that work?

➔ May I have a school calendar with information on _____ (holidays, vacations, **half-day sessions**, **snow days**).

➔ Do the students have _____ (lockers, **gym** lockers)?

➔ May I see the **playground**?

➔ What equipment is there _____ (on the playground, in the gym)?

➔ How old is the equipment?

Phrases for Learning About Your New School: Eating

➔ Does the school have a cafeteria that serves lunch? May I send lunch with my child?

➔ My child is _____ (allergic to peanuts, a vegetarian, a **picky eater**).

→ Do some children go home for lunch?

→ Is there a **buddy system** for new students so during lunch they aren't eating alone?

→ Are there **staggered** lunch periods?

Phrases for Discussing Problems in School

→ My child was in a **Montessori school** in our country and is not used to this type of learning.

→ My son/daughter is finding it difficult to **adjust to** your school.

→ My son/daughter needs help.

→ I'm concerned about _____ (difficulties with home-work, problems socializing with other students, **isolation**, **bullying**).

→ What do you suggest to help parents **cope** during these difficult **transitional times**, especially parents with limited English?

→ We are concerned about drug and alcohol use among young children. What are the school's **preventive measures** against these problems?

→ Please tell us about your school's **policies** on _____ (bullying, alcohol use, drug prevention).

Phrases for Discussing Problems in School: Bullying and Safety

→ I understand bullying is a major issue in the United States. How do you control it?

→ How is bullying dealt with by the _____ (students, teachers, staff)?

→ Could you share the policy for treating the _____ (**bully**, victim)?

→ Are there **monitors** in the halls and restrooms?

Phrases for Speaking with the Teacher and Other School Personnel

→ I would like to set up an appointment to discuss my _____ (child's, son's, daughter's) progress.

→ I would like to schedule a parent-teacher _____ (meeting, conference).

→ Are you available _____ (before school, after school, during the school day)?

→ Please call _____ (me at home at [your phone number], my cell phone at [your cell phone number]).

→ Please e-mail me at _____ (your e-mail address).

→ Please contact me as soon as possible about dates and times so I may _____ (adjust my schedule, arrange for transportation, clear my calendar, get babysitting for my other children). Thank you.

Phrases You May Hear While Visiting a New School

→ We send **report cards** out with the children to bring home _____ (every **marking period**, every six weeks).

→ Classes begin at 9 a.m.

→ In an emergency, what is the best way to contact you?

→ Here is a list of supplies that all new students need.

→ We have a **fire drill** every semester.

→ Don't worry about the noise; it's just a fire drill.

→ I'm sorry about the condition of the _____ (parking lot, halls, restrooms); the **custodian** is out sick today.

→ I can meet with you about your son/daughter on Monday morning at 8:00, before classes start.

→ If you wait until **recess** is over, we can speak about this more.

You will have other choices of schools in which to enroll your children: private schools, including Montessori schools, **Waldorf schools**, and **charte**r **schools**. Some parents even **opt** for **homeschooling**. The phrases in this chapter are also helpful in investigating these choices. Since the investigation process is time and energy consuming, your child may begin in the public school in your area, and you or they may elect to change later. Your local library can help with the **legwork** in getting information on these alternatives.

Phrases Specific to Middle School and High School Students

➜ Are there any sessions to help me prepare for college? What are they?

➜ Does this state have any **college fairs** for me to attend?

➜ Are there certain **elective courses** I should be taking?

➜ How may I use the summers to prepare for college?

➜ I don't _____ (want to, plan to, need to) attend college for my future career.

➜ I want to study _____ (**music producing**, TV news reporting, weather forecasting).

➜ How can I find out more about _____ (these fields, **technical schools**)?

➜ How about **internships**? Do you know of any in the field I want to enter?

➜ I'd like to speak to former graduates who have entered _____ (these fields, these technical schools, these colleges/universities). Can you **put me in touch with** them? You may give them my _____ (name, e-mail address, cell phone number).

➜ Would you be able to _____ (recommend me, give me a recommendation, write me a **letter of recommendation**)?

➜ What courses do I still have to take? Is there any **way around** taking statistics?

→ Do you think a tutor could help me? Could you recommend one? Thanks.

→ What about applying for _____ (**financial aid**, **scholarships**, **work-study programs**)?

Idioms and Other Vocabulary

Adjust to: get used to

Buddy system: putting together two students—a new one with one who has experience and can make it easier for the new student

Bully: person who engages in bullying another person (The person being threatened is called the victim.)

Bullying: threatening, frightening someone because the person is different

Change classes: move from class to class for different subjects (math, science, etc.) instead of being in one room with one teacher for most subjects

Charter schools: schools that have been given state government money to operate but are not operated by the public school system

College fairs: gatherings of students interested in attending college after high school for them to get information from school representatives

Comprise: contain within oneself

Cope: handle, take care of

Counselor: a person whose job is to help people with problems

Custodian: a person whose job is to take care of keeping a building, such as a school, in order

Cutoff date: date when something stops

Discouraged: not looked upon as a good idea

Dropouts: students who stop attending high school before they graduate

Elective courses: classes you may choose to take after taking all required classes

Equivalent to: equal to, the same as

ESL, ESOL: English as a Second Language, English for Speakers of Other Languages

Financial aid: money loaned or granted to students from a governmental body or other organization for college or university education

Fire drill: a practice session on how to leave the school if there is a fire

GED: general equivalency diploma, received by students who don't finish high school but study what they would have studied in high school and pass a test on that material

Gym: short for gymnasium, a special location with equipment for physical activity and sports

Half-day sessions: days when there is only a half day of school for various reasons, such as a teachers' meeting or special celebration

Homeschooling: teaching children at home, not in school

Internships: work programs for students to get experience in a field of study

Isolation: being kept separate from other students

Legwork: traveling to get work accomplished

Letter of recommendation: letter saying someone has the qualities to be good at a job or in a school

Mainstreamed: made part of a regular class

Mandatory: required

Marking period: amount of time in a school year at the end of which grades are issued

Monitors: people, sometimes children, whose job is to watch for trouble

Montessori school: school offering an alternative educational approach

Music producing: job that involves the overall control of the preparation of music production

Opt: choose, select

Options: choices

Picky eater: person who is very particular about what he or she likes to eat

Playground: area outside a school used for physical activity and sports

Plus (*n*): an advantage, an edge

Policies: systems of actions required in different situations

Preventive measures: actions to stop undesirable things from happening

Psychosocial: related to the mind and behavior, interpersonal

Pull-out classes: special training provided to students outside of their mainstream classes

Put me in touch with: connect me to

Reading: training to read more efficiently or working on reading conditions such as dyslexia where letters or words are read incorrectly

Recess: time of rest during the school day

Red tape: rules that slow down efforts to get things done

Report cards: teachers' written reports about students' school-work, which are sent home for parents to read and sign

Reverse: change to do in the opposite way

Scholarships: money given by an organization to help pay for education

Shortcuts: ways to do things faster

Shy: not comfortable speaking with strangers and, sometimes, people you've met

Snow days: days where there is too much snow to attend school

Source: a good location

Speech: special training in correct speaking

Staggered: arranged so that people are not all doing something at the same time

Technical schools (*also* **technical colleges**): schools where students, who have completed high school or earned a GED, concentrate on learning and doing, especially creating, building, or repairing objects and equipment

Transitional times: times of change from one situation to another

Waldorf schools: schools offering an alternative approach to education

Way around: way to not have to do something

Work-study programs: work that students do at a college or university to help pay for their expenses

CHAPTER 3

Furthering Your Own Education

E ducation for children in the United States offers many choices, but what many **fail to realize** is that in the United States, very many adults take courses to **advance** their careers or **simply** for **enrichment** or **enjoyment**.

Adult Education

There are classes for adults in high schools, junior colleges, colleges, universities, and churches. Private educational companies as well as advanced educational institutions offer courses online as well as training **via Skype**. You may work toward a certificate, a diploma, a degree, or a license. You may go just to enjoy yourself, meet people with similar interests, and practice your English communication and listening comprehension skills while you learn.

The choices are **staggering**, and searching online may be **daunting** at first. It can be an exciting "**field trip**" to go to your local library in order to investigate the educational and pleasurable learning possibilities available to you. The library staff can greatly help you as you start your search. There are many courses, classes, presentations, trips, and tours offered by your library or other nearby libraries, and a library is a good place to **get your feet wet**. Many offerings at the libraries are free of charge.

Subjects offered are as diverse as **auto mechanics**, classical-music appreciation, **line dancing**, astronomy, English and practically every other language, and cooking foods from every country **imaginable**. Offerings may be free, or there may be free **trial classes** to decide if you **relate to** the material and the presenter. For other classes, you may have to pay tuition, enrollment fees, and a fee for each hour of course credit. The specific amounts vary from school to school.

It may be a **challenge** to take a course in English, even if it focuses on your field of work or study or is similar to one you have taken already in your native language. You would have the knowledge in the area but not yet in the language. You might take a course about your religion or about your country and contribute your knowledge and ideas, although in limited English. (See Chapter 4, "Language Training.")

There are film classes in which the students watch a movie together in the classroom or separately at home and then discuss it in the class. The discussion might be among the students themselves, or else one of the actors, the director, or a film critic might conduct the discussion. Book clubs work in a similar **fashion**: the participants read the same book or author and meet to discuss their

takes on the particular reading selection. Some courses include trips or tours to interesting sites and lectures about the locations.

Another **avenue** to look into is **Toastmasters International**. Some companies offer this group to their employees, but there are also public Toastmasters groups that meet in restaurants or other venues. They concentrate on speaking and presentation skills as well as leadership skills. Belonging to the groups is very inexpensive. You may attend a meeting to see if your level of language skills and commitment to the **regimen** are enough for this wonderful organization.

Sports and games are another area to investigate. One of my students from China was **depressed** because he had no **outlet** other than his work and study. I asked him what he liked to do in his country. He said he would never be able to find that sport in the United States. Being curious, I **pursued** my line of questioning until he admitted to being a volleyball **enthusiast**. We looked on the Internet and found a volleyball group that met every evening of the week within a few miles of where this man lived. He was **shy** about going, but he went and continued in the group, going three times a week. There are many stories like this one, and the possibilities are **endless**.

An **innovative** area to investigate online, by **word of mouth**, or just through people you meet at your children's school, at the library, or **elsewhere** is a language exchange. People also post notices on supermarket **bulletin boards** for these services: "Language Exchange: I would like to learn/practice my English skills with a native American English speaker in exchange for speaking/ teaching _____ (Portuguese, Spanish, Vietnamese, [your language]) to that person. We could meet at this market, a library, or a coffee shop. Please call my cell for more details."

Phrases You May Hear About Adult Education

→ This _____ (course, class, session) _____ (runs, meets, takes place) during the _____ (winter, spring, fall, summer).

→ This class meets in the evenings from 6 p.m. to 8 p.m.

→ The _____ (course, class, program, session) that you have chosen meets on _____ (Monday, Tuesday, Wednesday, Thursday, Friday, Saturday, Sunday) during the _____ (evenings, mornings, afternoons) from _____ (time) to _____ (time).

→ We offer child care facilities in the student center.

→ _____ (Babysitting, Child care) is _____ (included in, part of) the _____ (fee, cost, price).

→ This is a "**lunch and learn**" class. Bring a sandwich, and a beverage will be supplied.

→ We encourage you to **audit** a class.

Phrases to Ask About Adult Education

→ Who teaches this _____ (class, course, group of sessions, event)?

→ Who leads this session?

→ What are the _____ (particulars, specifics, highlights) of this?

→ Can you _____ (e-mail, send, forward) me the details?

→ Where does the group meet? When does the group meet?

→ Where are the sessions _____ (held, taking place)?

→ When are the classes _____ (scheduled for, taking place)?

→ Can you give me directions?

→ How much does this cost? What is the cost?

→ Are _____ (materials, books, videos, CDs, DVDs) included, or are they _____ (extra, additional)?

→ May I _____ (audit, observe, sit in on) the sessions? I am shy about my English skills.

→ What if my English is not good? May I _____ (audit, still take, sit in on) this program? I'm interested in the subject and would like to hear what is being said.

→ Can I try out the class?

→ Could I observe one time before I **commit**?

→ Is a free trial lesson available?

→ I was a(n) _____ (engineer, musician, science teacher) in my country, and I want to keep up with the subject.

→ Do you have _____ (an application, more information) that you can send me?

→ Do I have to _____ (register, enroll, pay) now, or may I do that _____ (when I go to the first session, after the first class)?

Idioms and Other Vocabulary

Advance: move ahead

Audit: sit in on a class without getting a grade

Auto mechanics: lessons about how to fix your car

Avenue: direction

Bulletin boards: board on a wall on which you can put notes

Challenge: difficult task

Commit: promise to do

Daunting: challenging, difficult

Depressed: sad

Elsewhere: in other places

Endless: so long that it seems there is no end

Enjoyment: the experience of getting pleasure out of something or getting fun from something

Enrichment: process of making better

Enthusiast: person who is extremely interested in an activity

Fail to realize: don't understand

Fashion: way, manner

Field trip: a short visit to a place of interest

Get your feet wet: get started

Imaginable: possible to think of

Innovative: new, different, unusual

Line dancing: type of dancing performed by a group of people standing in a line

Lunch and learn: describing classes taken during a lunchtime break

Outlet: way to use physical and emotional energy

Pursued: continued

Regimen: special plan

Relate to: get along with, like

Shy: not comfortable talking to strangers

Simply: only

Skype: service for communicating via the computer, using an attached camera and microphone so that people can see and hear each other

Staggering: unbelievable

Takes (*n*): thoughts about a subject

Toastmasters International: international speakers' club with many groups around the world offering meetings where members practice speaking and leadership skills

Trial classes: classes you are trying out to see whether or not you like them

Via: by way of

Word of mouth: getting a message by hearing someone talking

CHAPTER 4

Language Training

An English-language learner has many options for increasing his or her fluency in the language. The first thing to realize is that the world is your classroom, with as many chances to **absorb** and practice new expressions as there are situations in your daily life. Be more **ambitious** in your language **use** than native speakers, who **typically** use only a fraction of their vocabulary in everyday speech! Also, **recognize** that your native **tongue** is a valuable **commodity**. Many English speakers **envy** your bilingualism and **long to** learn a foreign language. As mentioned in Chapter 3, **propose** a language **exchange** or **barter** with someone whose English you admire and who would like to learn your language. Make sure that the person speaks American English and not British English. Also, the more idioms the person uses, the better the casual conversation becomes.

Half an hour for each language over coffee could help both of you make real progress and create a new friendship.

A more structured **approach** might be preferable, especially if you are in the early stage of learning English. ESL or ESOL classes are easy to find, but deciding which one is best for you may be more difficult. Universities, colleges, community colleges, high school adult evening programs, language schools, libraries, and language companies all offer programs in English. Churches or other religious institutions also provide space for classes, and there are always private tutors. Each of these **options** has advantages; select the one that is most convenient and affordable to you at this time. You may always decide that what works now is not the best option for later, but get started!

Whatever option you choose for beginning your language training, it is important to realize that the time you spend between lessons is probably more **crucial** than the time spent at the lesson, as valuable as the lesson is. To justify the time and money spent on the classes (even if they may be free), you must study, practice, and use the language you learn between the classes. You are, **in essence**, responsible for your own progress. Use every bit of the language you learn to increase your **acquisition** of more of the **target language**. My neighbor from Goa, India, speaks English beautifully. When I asked him how he learned English, he said, "Well, the plane trip here was 23 hours, and I spoke to the people in the seats next to me all that time." He was, of course, exaggerating to make a point, but it is a point well taken. He took the risk to use limited language to gain more language.

Phrases You May Hear While Investigating Language-Learning Opportunities

→ There is a required _____ (entrance test, placement exam, interview).

→ We have a required textbook for this class.

→ The _____ (tuition, application fee, hourly rate, four-session rate, cost for a semester) is _____ (on the flyer, in this application form, on our website, based on a **sliding scale**, discussed during our **free pre-assessment session**).

→ There _____ (is, is not) a prerequisite for the class.

→ Once you decide to _____ (join, enroll, sign up), there are no auditors.

→ Please come in and sit in on one of the classes.

→ Please come and _____ (see our **facility**, take a tour).

→ The class meets _____ (once a week for two hours, three times a week for three hours, five days a week from 10 a.m. to 1 p.m.).

→ The semester starts in _____ (February, May). We also offer a summer program.

→ This is not a bilingual class; everything is done in the target language, English, but at your level so you will definitely be able to handle it.

→ There are special classes in listening comprehension.

→ There are _____ (three levels, six levels).

→ This is _____ (spring, Christmas, summer) **break**, but let's schedule an appointment for you to come in the week after the break.

→ We are having an **orientation** _____ (next week, in February, Friday). Can you join us to meet and observe?

Phrases You May Say While Investigating Language-Learning Opportunities

→ What level of language ability is required for this class?

→ Is this a(n) _____ (mixed-level class, beginners group, intermediate-level class, advanced class)?

→ Will this be _____ (one-to-one private, a small group, a full class session)?

→ My native first language is _____ (your language).

→ Are there any instructors who specialize in teaching English to speakers of that language?

→ Does anyone here speak _____ (your language)?

→ I _____ (am looking for, would like to take) an accent modification program.

→ Do you think I can _____ (lose, correct, reduce, modify) my accent?

→ I have been told that I speak _____ (very quickly, too fast, too softly). What do you think?

→ I came to the United States _____ (at 10 years old, at 19 years old, two years ago and I am 30).

→ Since this will be _____ (one-to-one, private), where will we meet?

→ Can we meet at the library?

→ Where is your office? Could you please e-mail me
_____ (directions, the address)?

→ Please mail the syllabus to me, since classes don't start for a month.

→ Do you take _____ (checks, credit cards, debit cards, cash)?

Phrases You May Say to Ensure Understanding

→ Please _____ (spell that, repeat that, say that again).

→ I'm sorry, I didn't _____ (understand, get, **catch**) that.

→ Could you _____ (say that more slowly, send it to me in an e-mail)?

→ Is it difficult to _____ (understand, hear) me over the telephone?

→ You did say next month, didn't you?

→ Do you mean next Wednesday?

→ Excuse me, I don't really _____ (**follow you**, understand you).

→ Pardon me. Could you please tell me how this private tutoring **arrangement** is going to work?

Idioms and Other Vocabulary

Absorb: take in

Acquisition: what you get

Ambitious: determined to get ahead

Approach: plan

Arrangement: what is planned

Barter: exchange, trade

Break: rest period from some activity

Catch: get, understand

Commodity: item

Crucial: very important

Envy: wish to have

Exchange: trade, barter

Facility: place, building

Follow you: understand you

Free pre-assessment session: no-charge time in which you make a judgment before formal testing

In essence: pointing out an important idea

Long to: strongly wish to

Options: choices

Orientation: outlining of a program

Propose: suggest

Recognize: realize that it is important

Sliding scale: payment system in which the amount to pay for services depends on certain conditions

Target language: language you are studying, language you want to learn

Tongue: language

Typically: usually

Use (*n*): what you do with something

Part 1 Notes

PART 2

Health and Medical Situations

Active Learning Advice: Make Friends

Make friends—American friends or friends whose native language is different from yours. To do this, it will be necessary to communicate with each other in English. It will be difficult at first, but each time you meet, it will get easier. Start with a short, friendly visit of maybe five minutes, and then meet for a little longer each time you get together.

Where can you meet these friends?

- At work
- At your church, synagogue, mosque, or other place of **worship**
- At a gym, health club, or spa
- At a supermarket, grocery store, butcher **shop**, **produce** market, **farmers' market**, **flea market**, **garage sale**, or **house sale**
- At your child's school, playground, **after-school activity**, or **PTA** or **PTO** meetings
- In an ESL, computer, music appreciation, or any other class that may be of interest to you
- In your neighborhood, where you live or work

- At a **volunteer** or charitable organization, donating your time and help
- On a bus, train, subway, or airplane

Practice speaking English **out loud** (**aloud**) with yourself. It will help you to have better conversations with other people. Listen to conversations others have—on TV, at work, or in any of the other places listed. What do you like? Use it. What don't you understand? Ask or look it up.

Friendly Hint

There is a difference between a friend and an acquaintance. Forming friendships takes time. An acquaintance is someone you have met who may never be a friend or has not become a friend yet. That doesn't mean you can't practice saying, "Hi, nice to see you again. I saw you at the last PTA meeting."

Chatting and small talk are terms for light conversations that are not about anything serious. You may say, "The weather is really cold this winter." You don't have to add a time and place for another meeting or anything more than a short comment.

Idioms and Other Vocabulary

After-school activity: something to do after classes for interest or fun, such as sports or special-interest clubs

Farmers' market: a market where farmers sell their fruits and vegetables directly to customers

Flea market: a market where old, used, and low-priced new items are sold

Garage sale: a sale of used items from someone's home held outside of the home in a garage, driveway, or yard

House sale: a sale of furniture and other items in a home, usually when someone is moving or has died and the family is emptying the home

Out loud (*also* **aloud**): to say or read in a normal voice but not silently or to yourself

Produce: fruits or vegetables

PTA, PTO: Parent-Teacher Association, Parent-Teacher Organization (Schools have one of these groups so parents and teachers can communicate, have meetings, and offer activities for the benefit of the school and the students.)

Shop: small store

Volunteer: involving people who offer time and talent for no payment

Worship: religious activity showing respect for a god or gods

CHAPTER 5

Making and Keeping a Medical Appointment

When you need to have medical care, even for something **minor**, it is important to **do your homework**. To get **recommendations**, **check with** neighbors, **colleagues** (if you are working), or a **referral service** at a local hospital. The service will give you **a few** referrals and information about the doctors' education and training.

If you go to one doctor and don't **feel comfortable** with that doctor or with his or her **office staff**, you then have other **choices**. You are the **consumer**, the **patient**.

Medical professionals want to help you, and you have to help them to help you by giving them all the information you can. Bring all your **past medical records** (translated if possible), x-rays/films, medical test results, list of medications you are taking, including vitamins, and anything else you think can help **explain** your **concerns**. **Supply whatever** will help the doctor understand your **issues** and be able to help you better. Also, write down all your questions, ask them, and get them answered.

When you call to make an appointment with a doctor, the telephone may be **picked up** by voice mail. Or you may reach the receptionist or a nurse without going into a voice mail system.

Phrases You May Hear on Voice Mail When You Call a Doctor's Office

→ If this is an emergency, **hang up** the phone and call 9-1-1.

→ If you want to _____

    → make an appointment,

    → change or cancel an existing appointment,

    → discuss billing,

    → have insurance questions **addressed**,

    → get test results,

    → hear office hours,

    → get directions to our office,

    → speak to the **receptionist**,

    → speak with a nurse,

→ press _____ (1, 2, 3, 4, 5, 6, 7, 8, 9, or 0 for operator).

Phrases You May Hear When a Person Answers the Telephone

→ Good morning. Dr. Smith's office.

→ How may I _____ (help, assist, be of service to) you?

→ Is this an emergency?

→ Is this a _____ (**sick visit**, **well visit**, first visit, regular appointment, checkup)?

→ Have you been to this office before? When?

→ Could you please **hold on** for one moment?

→ Could you kindly wait a minute? I'll find a nurse for you.

→ Could you please **call back during office hours**?

→ Who recommended _____ (us, this office, Dr. _____) to you? Is he/she a patient?

→ What _____ (health, medical, **supplemental**) insurance do you have?

→ What _____ (is the problem, seems to be the issue, is bothering you, is wrong, is troubling you)?

→ **What is the matter?**

→ I'm sorry, _____ I didn't (understand, **get that**, **catch** what you said). Could you please _____ (repeat, speak more slowly, say that again, **spell** that for me, spell that name again)?

Phrases You May Hear When Making an Appointment

➜ The doctor can see you _____ (Monday, Tuesday, Wednesday, Thursday, Friday, Saturday, tomorrow, next week).

➜ What time works best for you?

➜ Is morning or afternoon better?

➜ Is _____ (first thing in the morning, after lunch, 9:30 a.m., 2 p.m., the first appointment, the last appointment of the day) good for you?

➜ Please bring _____ (your insurance card, your insurance information, your medical history, a photo ID, your birth certificate, your passport, a current green card).

➜ Please bring an adult who speaks your language and English.

Pronunciation: Days of the Week

Monday	/Munday/
Tuesday	/Toozday/
Wednesday	/Wenzday/
Thursday	/Therzday/
Friday	/Fryday/
Saturday	/Saterday/
Sunday	/Sunday/

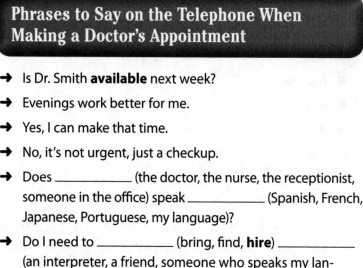

Phrases to Say on the Telephone When Making a Doctor's Appointment

→ Is Dr. Smith **available** next week?

→ Evenings work better for me.

→ Yes, I can make that time.

→ No, it's not urgent, just a checkup.

→ Does _____ (the doctor, the nurse, the receptionist, someone in the office) speak _____ (Spanish, French, Japanese, Portuguese, my language)?

→ Do I need to _____ (bring, find, **hire**) _____ (an interpreter, a friend, someone who speaks my language and English)?

→ I prefer to be examined by a female doctor.

Writing Dates in the United States

When the doctor's office gives you an appointment, remember how dates are written in the United States: the month first, the day next, and the year last. The 23rd day of April in the year 2011 could be written April 23, 2011, or 4/23/11. In many other countries, this date would be written with the day before the month: 23 April 2011 or 23/4/11.

Describing Aches and Pains

There are five parts of the body in which the word *ache* (pronounced /ake/) can be attached as part of the word:

- A backache
- An earache (*an* because ear begins with a vowel [a, e, i, o, u])
- A headache
- A stomachache (pronounced /stomikake/)—children also call it a bellyache or tummy ache
- A toothache

You can also say, "I have a pain in my _____ (back, ear, head, stomach, tooth)." You may also say, "I have a sore _____ (back, ear, head, stomach, tooth)." Another way to say this is, "My _____ (back, ear, head, stomach, tooth) hurts."

Some ailments or illnesses are used with *a* or *the*. For example, say, "I have a sore throat"; "I have a fever"; "I have a temperature"; "He has a cold"; "She has the flu."

Phrases to Say in the Doctor's Office or When Describing an Ailment

→ Where should I wait for the doctor?

→ Do I need to fill out a new-patient form?

→ I have a/an/the _____.

   → stomachache

   → headache

   → backache

   → toothache

→ earache

→ **sore throat**

→ **fever**

→ cold

→ flu

→ Should I stay in the _____ (**waiting room**, **examination room**, doctor's office)?

→ I have a _____ (pain, **lump**) in my _____ (shoulder, hip, knee, back, stomach, toe).

→ I have a _____ (sore, **bruise**, **rash**) on my _____ (chest, back, arm, leg, stomach).

→ This has been _____ (**bothering** me, hurting, aching, **annoying** me) for _____ (a few days, a week, a couple of weeks).

Phrases for Clarifying a Diagnosis

→ What is the **diagnosis**?

→ What is my problem?

→ What is (**wrong** with me, **the matter** with me)?

→ What is the **prognosis**?

→ What do I need to do?

→ What is this **condition** called?

→ What is the **next step**?

→ **Where does this come from?**

→ What should I do to keep this condition **under control**?

→ Do you have any _____ (written information, **pamphlets**) about this condition?

→ Do you have any **sample medications** for this condition?

→ Are there any **side effects** with this medication?

→ Are there **interactions** with other drugs I'm taking?

→ Do I need to get an appointment with a **specialist**?

→ Do I need to get _____ (a **second opinion**, another opinion)?

→ Please, could you _____ (say that again, explain that more slowly)?

→ Please, could you give me more information?

→ I am **nervous** about this.

→ I am **unfamiliar** with this condition.

→ I am not clear about what you are saying.

→ I am **confused**.

→ I am not fluent in English. Please repeat what you said.

Phrases You May Hear from the Doctor or Nurse

→ What medications are you taking?

→ Are you **allergic** to _____ (any medications, any foods, any materials like **latex** or **adhesive**)?

→ Do you have any **allergies**?

→ Are you pregnant?

→ Do you have _____ (an **advance directive**, a **living will**, a **power of attorney**)?

→ Who is your **next of kin**?

→ Please _____ (take, have the pharmacy fill) this **prescription**.

→ Here are some **samples** of the medication I _____ (want you to take, have prescribed for you, think will help you, feel will **relieve** your **symptoms**).

→ Please call the office to tell me/us how the medication is working.

→ Please call the office to make a **follow**-**up appointment**.

→ See the receptionist _____ (before you leave, on the way out, at the desk) to _____ (make a follow-up appointment, pick up sample medication to **get started**, pay your **co-pay**).

Idioms and Other Vocabulary

A few: not many of something you can count

Addressed: paid attention to, answered

Adhesive: a sticky substance used to make some medical products (bandages)

Advance directive (*also* **living will**): a legal paper that details your wishes if you should become unable to make serious medical decisions

Allergic: becoming sick when using a particular medicine, eating a particular food, or using a particular product

Allergies: reactions you have when exposed to a substance you are allergic to

Annoying: making you feel uncomfortable

Available: freed up to do one's job/work

Bothering: disturbing, annoying, hurting

Bruise: mark or discoloration on the skin

Call back during office hours: make this call again when the office is open

Catch: hear or understand

Check with: get information from

Choices: places where you feel more comfortable or better helped

Colleagues: people you work with

Concerns: what is worrying or bothering you

Condition: disease or medical issue

Confused: not clear about, don't understand

Consumer: person who uses the services

Co-pay: the patient's/insured's share of the cost of the appointment

Diagnosis: decision about what is wrong or what the medical problem is

Do your homework: prepare, get ready

Examination room: room where the doctor looks at and talks to you about your medical issues

Explain: make clear

Feel comfortable: think this is the place for you

Fever: a higher than normal (98.6°F in the U.S.) temperature

Follow-up appointment: another appointment after this one

Get started: to begin

Get that: understand that, hear that

Hang up: end the phone call

Hire: give paid employment to

Hold on: don't hang up the telephone

Interactions: effects of one medication on another medication

Issues: problems

Latex: a substance used in making doctors' rubber examination gloves

Living will: (*see* **Advance directive**)

Lump: small hard area under the skin

Medical professionals: people trained in the field of medicine, including doctors, nurses, and other people involved in medical care

Minor: relatively unimportant

Nervous: worried about, not relaxed

Next of kin: closest living relative(s)

Next step: the thing to do after this

Office staff: nurses, technicians, receptionists, people who work in doctors' offices

Pamphlets: Folded or stapled paper with brief information

Past medical records: reports from doctors and hospitals in your country

Patient: a person who gets medical treatment

Picked up: answered the telephone

Power of attorney: written document giving authority to a person you have chosen to sign legal papers for you if you become unable to do so yourself

Prescription: form written by a doctor ordering medication from a pharmacy

Prognosis: what the doctor predicts will happen in the future with this disease or illness

Rash: reddish discoloration of the skin

Receptionist: a person who has the job to welcome people who come to the doctor's office

Recommendations: people saying you should go to or use this doctor

Referral service: service to help people select or choose doctors or other medical services

Relieve: to ease pain or problems

Sample medications (*also* **samples**): free medication a doctor can give you until you get to a pharmacy with your prescription (These are often given to the doctor by pharmaceutical reps—people who represent the drug companies.)

Second opinion: advice of another doctor about this issue

Sick visit: doctor's visit when you are sick (ill) and need fast care

Side effects: negative reactions from a drug that is helping make your sickness better

Specialist: a doctor who treats only a certain disease or area of the body

Spell: say the letters of a word in order

Sore throat: pain and redness in the throat (passageway in back of the mouth leading to the stomach)

Supplemental: added to other, regular insurance

Supply: give, offer

Symptoms: physical issues that accompany an illness or injury

The matter: wrong, the problem

Under control: taken care of, being treated with success

Unfamiliar: new, different, not what you know

Waiting room: room where patients wait to be called in to see the doctor

Well visit: doctor's visit when you are not sick (ill) to check on your general health

What is the matter? (*sounds like* /**whatsamata/**): What's wrong?

Whatever: anything you have that is needed

Where does this come from?: How did I get this problem?

Wrong: not good, not right

CHAPTER 6

Making and Keeping
a Dental Appointment

Probably nobody likes to go to the dentist, but probably everyone knows that if you need a dentist in an emergency situation, the pain can be **unbearable**. Therefore, it is important to **line up** a dental **practice** or a dental care provider before you really need one. Again, if you are new to the United States, rule one is to ask a friend, a neighbor, a colleague, or a dental referral service for recommendations. The health care benefits at your place of work may include a dental program that lists local dentists. There are also referral services such as 1-800-Dentist and Angie's List. Be **aware** when you call that some services charge for joining before giving referrals.

Vocabulary Hint: Terms for People

Nobody = not one person

Everybody = each and every person

Somebody = one person (Somebody, call the dentist.)

Anybody = one person (question form for *somebody*: Didn't anybody call the dentist?)

Also used: no one, everyone, someone, anyone.

All these words are singular and take the singular forms of verbs: Everyone is here. Nobody cares.

Phrases to Use to Find a Dental Office or Dentist

→ Can you recommend a good dentist?

→ Could you recommend a dentist you're happy with?

→ I would like to find a dentist in my area.

→ I would like to find a dentist for my child.

→ I'm looking for a dental hygienist in my city.

→ I need to find a dentist for _____ (an appointment, a cleaning, an emergency, my child).

→ I _____ (don't have, have) dental insurance.

You can tell a lot from a regular cleaning appointment at a dentist's office—about the dentist, the hygienist, the staff, the office space itself, and the condition of the equipment. If you aren't comfortable with any of these, you may decide to try another dental office before continuing if/when you need more-involved dental work.

Phrases to Say on the Telephone Before the Dental Appointment

→ Yes, I will bring my dental records.

→ Yes, I can bring my previous x-rays.

→ I have my insurance card and a photo ID.

→ I can send for my documents.

→ Is there any other information from my dentist in _____ (your country) that you _____ (need, have to have translated)?

Phrases to Say About Insurance

→ I _____ (have, do not have) dental insurance.

→ My policy is with _____ (name of your insurance company), and my policy number is _____ (policy number on your insurance card).

→ Do you accept this insurance?

→ Is there a **co-pay**, or will you accept what my insurance pays?

→ If you don't accept my insurance, how much is _____ (a dental checkup, an x-ray, a cleaning)?

→ Since you don't accept my insurance, could you **recommend** _____ (a **clinic**, a **dental school**, a dentist who might accept my insurance), please?

Grammar Hint: *Tooth* (One) vs. *Teeth* (More than One)

You always say "toothache," never "teethache," even if more than one tooth hurts. If more than one tooth hurts, you say, "My teeth ache."

It's always *toothpaste*, never teethpaste, and *toothbrush*, never teethbrush.

Say, "I have a toothache," or "My tooth hurts," or "My tooth **aches**," or "I have a pain in my tooth," or "My teeth hurt," or "My teeth ache."

Phrases to Describe Your Problem

→ I need a dental checkup.

→ I need a cleaning.

→ When may I make an appointment?

→ I have a _____ (slight, bad, very bad) **toothache**.

→ My **tooth hurts**.

→ My **teeth** ache.

→ My **gums** are bleeding.

→ My tongue is **swollen**.

→ My **jaw** is **sore**.

→ I have trouble _____ (chewing, biting, biting down).

→ I have a problem with eating cold foods.

→ I experience discomfort drinking hot drinks.

→ My gums are sensitive.

→ I have discomfort when I swallow.

→ I have a problem **swallowing**.

→ I grind my teeth when I sleep.

→ At night, I **bite** the inside of my mouth.

→ I feel pain in my jaw when I wake up.

Phrases You May Hear from the Dentist

→ When was your last _____ (dental appointment, cleaning, visit to a dentist)?

→ Where was this appointment?

→ Did you have dental _____ (x-rays, films) taken?

→ Are you pregnant?

→ Do you have your _____ (x-rays, films, dental records) with you?

→ Please _____ (open, open **wide**, open your mouth).

→ Please turn your face (**toward** me, away from me).

→ Please open your mouth more.

→ Please _____ (close, close your mouth, close a little).

→ Now you can _____ (**rinse**, **spit** into the **basin**, spit into the bowl, take some water and rinse out your mouth).

→ Please **point to** where the **pain** is.

→ Show me where it hurts.

→ **Touch** where it is **tender**.

→ Does it hurt when you _____ (**chew**, **bite down**, drink hot/cold **beverages**)?

→ Do you want/need _____ (to be **put to sleep**, me to use **gas**, to be **injected** with **Novocain**) before I _____ (**drill**, **pull the tooth**, work on your gums, start the **root canal**)?

→ Are you allergic to _____ (any medications, anything)?

→ Have you ever had a **reaction to** Novocain?

→ I'd like you to see a(n) _____ (**periodontist**, **oral surgeon**, **prosthodontist**).

→ We'll give you _____ (a prescription for pain medication, a prescription for antibiotics, another appointment).

→ Here is _____ (a special toothbrush, toothpaste, **dental floss**, **mouthwash**).

Phrases to Use During the Dental Appointment

→ I need a cleaning.

→ Do I need x-rays?

→ I don't want x-rays, because I _____ (am/may be pregnant, just had them six months ago).

→ I have a _____ (terrible, bad, **slight**, constant) toothache.

→ The pain is _____ (constant, **intermittent**, **sharp**, **dull**).

→ This is where the pain is.

→ This is where it _____ (hurts, is tender, is sore, aches).

→ I have _____ (false teeth, a **bridge**, an upper bridge, a lower bridge, an **implant**, **veneers**).

→ I _____ (**am allergic to**, **have an allergy to**, have a reaction to) _____ (names of medications).

→ My _____ (jaw, mouth, lips, gums) are **numb**.

→ Will I need _____ (a root canal, a tooth pulled, a **cavity** filled, any other dental work)?

→ Will I need to _____ (come back, have a return visit)?

→ Do I need a prescription for _____ (pain, swelling, bleeding)?

→ Can you recommend an **orthodontist** for my _____ (child, son, daughter)?

→ My daughter's teeth are coming in crooked. I may need an orthodontist.

→ He/She may need _____ (**braces**, a **retainer**, orthodontic work).

→ Can you recommend a good **pedodontist** in the area?

Idioms and Other Vocabulary

Aches: dull, not sharp pains

Aware: have knowledge of

Basin: sink

Be allergic to (*also* **have an allergy to**): experience a negative reaction to food, medicine, material, etc.

Beverages: drinks—hot or cold, alcoholic or not

Bite (*also* **bite down**): press your teeth onto

Braces: wires used to straighten teeth

Bridge: artificial teeth connected with metal to other teeth in the mouth

Cavity: hole in a tooth caused by decay

Chew: bite down on many times

Clinic: place where dental work is done at a lower cost than at a private dentist

Co-pay: amount a patient with insurance must pay for dental work (The insurance pays for a portion of the dental work, and the patient pays the rest, the co-pay.)

Dental floss: strong, thin string used to clean between teeth

Dental school: a school where dentists study and do supervised dental work at a lower cost than a private dental office

Drill: use an electric tool for making holes in teeth

Dull: not severe, not very bad

Gas: chemical used to put someone to sleep during dental procedures

Gums: parts inside mouth that hold teeth

Hurts: gives pain

Implant: artificial tooth inserted into gum

Injected: put into the body with a needle

Intermittent: not constant

Jaw: bone of the lower face

Line up: arrange for

Mouthwash: liquid used to kill germs or bacteria and make mouth fresh

Novocain: drug used to take away feeling of pain during dental work

Numb: not able to feel pain

Oral surgeon: dentist who operates on the mouth or jaw

Orthodontist: dentist who straightens crooked teeth

Pain: feeling of hurt

Pedodontist: dentist specially trained to treat children

Periodontist: a dental specialist who works on gums

Point to: show with your finger

Practice: professional office

Probably: in most cases, often, more likely

Prosthodontist: dental specialist in replacement of missing teeth and restoration of natural teeth

Pull the tooth: take out the tooth with dental tools

Put to sleep: use gas during dental procedures

Reaction to: bad effect from e.g. skin rash

Recommend: advise

Retainer: object worn in the mouth to hold teeth in place

Rinse: use clean water to remove blood and dental solutions

Root canal: a dental procedure where the root of the tooth is treated and the tooth is not removed

Sharp: sudden and strong

Slight: very little

Sore: painful

Spit: empty your mouth of liquid that accumulates in your mouth

Swallowing: action of making food go down the throat

Swollen: enlarged because of infection or injury

Tender: hurts or is painful if touched

Tooth (*singular; plural is* **teeth**): (*see sidebar earlier in chapter*)

Toothache: (*see sidebar earlier in chapter*)

Touch: put finger or hand on

Toward: in the direction of

Unbearable: extremely bad or painful

Veneers: thin enamel layers used to cover teeth

Wide: very big from one side to the other

CHAPTER 7

Emergency Room and Hospital Care

Hopefully, you or your loved ones may never need emergency medical care or a hospital stay, but if you do, you must be prepared to communicate quickly, clearly, and effectively. Do not wait until an emergency to know and understand essential phrases.

In the United States, you dial 9-1-1 on the telephone to reach an emergency operator who can coordinate help for you. The number you call is pronounced "nine-one-one," not "nine-eleven." To Americans and many others, "nine eleven" refers to the date of September (the ninth month) 11, 2001, when terrorists attacked the World Trade Center towers in New York City and the Pentagon in Washington, DC.

If you hear "Call 9-1-1!" it means to call those numbers on a telephone.

Reasons to call 9-1-1 include police and fire emergencies, which are covered in Part 3, Chapters 12 and 13, as well as **true medical emergencies**. Don't **confuse** 9-1-1 with 4-1-1, which is for information—specifically, **finding out** telephone numbers—or 0 for operator, which is for telephone problems only.

Phrases You May Hear If You Call 9-1-1

→ What is your emergency?

→ Do you have a medical emergency?

→ What is your full name?

→ Are you injured?

→ Do you need an ambulance?

→ Are you _____?

  → bleeding

  → **dizzy**

  → ill

  → sick

  → **weak**

→ What is your **relationship** to the victim?

→ Is the **victim** breathing?

→ **Can he/she speak**?

→ Are his/her **airways blocked**? Look inside his/her mouth.

→ Do you know _____ (**mouth-to-mouth resuscitation, CPR**)?

→ Someone can talk you through these procedures, if you _____ (aren't sure about, don't know how to use) them.

→ Where are you?

→ What is your street address?

→ Do you know the **cross street**?

→ There is an **ambulance** on the way.

→ The **EMTs** will help you.

→ **Remain** at the **scene** until the emergency vehicle arrives.

→ Do not move the victim.

→ **Keep** the victim **warm**, if possible.

→ Where _____ (are you, is this emergency, is this happening)?

If you call 9-1-1, be **brief**. Say what you have to say and what the operator needs to hear in order to get you help as soon as possible. If a person who is fluent in English is with you, give him/her the phone, but don't take the time to go **look for** someone. Answer all the questions you are asked by the **professional** on the phone as best you can, and do what that person tells you to do until help arrives.

Phrases You Say if Calling 9-1-1

→ I need help!

→ Hurry, send help!

➜ This is an emergency!

➜ Please hurry!

➜ There has been _____ (an auto, a car, a motorcycle, a boating, a train, a swimming) accident.

➜ I have chest pains.

➜ I can't breathe.

➜ I have had an accident.

➜ I _____ (fell down the stairs and hurt my back, slipped on a wet floor and think I broke my arm).

➜ My daughter is choking.

➜ My son is choking on a piece of meat, and I can't get it out.

Sometimes people with serious medical issues go to the **emergency room** at a hospital **on their own**, **by themselves**, or by car if they are able to. There is **reserved** parking for the **emergency department**.

In the emergency room, patients are **treated**, after being **assessed**, in the order of the seriousness of their conditions. This method is called **triage**. Emergency rooms in hospitals are often very **crowded**, and you may have to wait **quite a while** before being seen by a nurse or doctor.

Phrases You May Hear in an Emergency Room or at a Reception Desk

➜ What happened?

➜ How did you get here?

→ Did you get here by ambulance?

→ Is someone with you? Can they take you home?

→ Should we get a translator for you?

→ Is there someone, a bilingual adult, who can translate for you?

→ The person who translates for you cannot be a child.

→ Have you ever been a patient in this hospital?

→ When were you a patient in this hospital?

→ Do you have _____ (medical insurance, **Medicare**, **Medicaid**)?

→ Are you **responsible for** the payment of the bills today?

→ Please _____ (**fill out**, **fill in**, **write**, **print**) _____ (all these papers, both sides of these forms, all the information, the lines highlighted, the information checked).

→ Sign all these forms.

→ We need your **signature** on these forms.

→ Do you have any questions?

→ Do you need to _____ (use our **Language Line**, call a bilingual friend or relative)?

→ Do you need us to find someone to _____ (**translate**, **interpret**, act as an interpreter, act as a translator) for you?

→ Who is your _____ (nearest, closest) _____ (relative, **blood relative**, family member)?

→ We need your _____ (consent, permission, written consent, signature) to _____ (examine, check, take blood from, medically test) you.

Phrases You May Hear from a Doctor or Nurse

→ Are you pregnant?

→ What medications are you on?

→ When was the last time you took these medications?

→ Do you have your medications with you?

→ Do you have a list of your medications?

→ Are you allergic to any medications?

→ Whatever you _____ (say, tell us, confide in us) will be _____ (private, confidential, released only with your permission).

→ The doctor has checked your _____ (test results, x-rays, blood tests).

→ The doctor would like to _____ (do more tests, consult with a **specialist**, keep you here).

→ I would like you to stay until we are sure that you are fully recovered.

→ We would like to treat you as _____ (an **outpatient**, an **inpatient**).

Phrases You May Hear When Leaving a Hospital

→ Everything _____ (is fine, checks out, seems in order).

→ You are free to go.

→ You may go home.

→ You can _____ (sign out, be released) from the hospital.

→ If you choose to leave, you must sign yourself out **AMA**.

→ Please wait for someone to take you _____ (to **admitting**, upstairs, downstairs, to the next step).

→ Do you have _____ (your car, a ride home)?

→ Is there someone _____ (with you, to drive you home)?

→ You came in an ambulance; do you need transportation home?

→ Should we _____ (call someone to pick you up, get a taxicab for you, make other arrangements)?

→ You will have to go downstairs in a **wheelchair** and with a _____ (nurse, aide, hospital employee).

The move from an emergency room to a hospital stay or even back home is a **traumatic transition**. You have been through an **ordeal** and may be nervous, frightened, scared, or worried. Certainly, you will be **worn out**. Sometimes being admitted to the hospital is a **precaution** or because of a minor issue. Remain positive and **calm**; this attitude could even improve your condition.

Idioms and Other Vocabulary

Admitting: hospital department where you/they fill out forms before you become a patient in a hospital

Airways blocked: breathing passages not clear

AMA: against medical advice

Ambulance: special vehicle used to take sick or hurt people to the hospital

Assessed: judged, decided on

Blood relative: a person related to you by birth

Breathing problems: trouble breathing without help

Brief: short

By oneself (*or* **myself,** *or* **yourself,** *or* **himself,** *or* **herself,** *or* **ourselves,** *or* **yourselves,** *or* **themselves**): alone

Calm: relaxed

Can speak: is able to talk after the injury or illness

Choking: unable to breathe

Confuse: mistake one thing and think it is a different thing

CPR (*see also* **mouth-to-mouth resuscitation**): cardiopulmonary resuscitation, breathing into the victim's mouth and pushing on his/her chest to restart breathing and the heart beating

Cross street: the street that meets your street at the corner and leads to and from your street

Crowded: filled with many people or things

Dizzy: feeling unbalanced, not steady on your feet

Emergency room (*also* **emergency department**): section of a hospital that treats patients who are seriously injured or sick

EMTs: emergency medical technicians

Fill in (*also* **fill out**): give written information asked for on a form

Finding out: getting information

Heart attack: condition when the heart stops working

Hemorrhaging: bleeding very heavily

Inpatient: a person staying in the hospital for at least one night

Interpret: change into another language (*Interpret* is for spoken language; *translate* is for written language.)

Keep warm: cover with a blanket, coat, or what you have

Language Line: service that makes interpreters and translators available on the telephone

Look for: try to locate

Medicaid: U.S. government program that helps pay for medical care for people without money to pay

Medicare: U.S. government program that helps pay for medical care for older people

Mouth-to-mouth resuscitation: part of CPR, breathing into someone's mouth to start up his/her breathing

On one's own: without help

Ordeal: very difficult situation

Outpatient: a person who comes to the hospital for an emergency or even for a surgery but goes home without staying overnight

Precaution: preventative action taken to stop something dangerous from happening

Print: put down letters one by one without joining or connecting them

Procedures: way of doing certain things

Professional: person trained to perform certain work

Quite a while: a lot of time

Relationship: connection, the way two people are connected

Remain: stay, don't leave

Reserved: saved for

Responsible for: in charge of

Scene: place where something happened

Signature: your name signed for legal papers

Specialist: doctor who treats one area of medicine or one disease (for example, a cardiologist treats heart disease, and a pulmonologist treats diseases of the lungs).

Stroke: illness in which blood in an artery stops moving

Talk you through: give you instructions in how to do something

Transition: change

Translate: change into another language (*Translate* is for written language; *interpret* is for spoken language.)

Traumatic: very disturbing

Treated: taken care of medically

Triage: system of giving emergency medical care according to the seriousness of the injury or illness

True medical emergencies: serious accidents or serious illness, such as heart attacks, strokes, choking, breathing problems, and hemorrhaging

Victim: person who is ill (sick) or very hurt

Weak: not physically strong

Wheelchair: a chair with wheels used to wheel someone who cannot or should not walk when leaving a hospital (After someone has been a patient, hospitals have a rule that they not walk or leave without a hospital employee.)

Worn out: very tired

Write: Form letters by hand that are attached, not printed separately

CHAPTER 8

The Pharmacy

I n the United States, the terms *pharmacy* and *drugstore* are used **interchangeably. Formerly**, a pharmacy prepared medications, and a drugstore **dispensed** them. Now many supermarkets also have pharmacies that fill prescriptions. Pharmacies and/or drugstores sell **over-the-counter** medicines, **administer inoculations**, and sell toys, candy, cosmetics, and numerous other articles as well as filling physicians' prescriptions. This may be different from the chemist shop or apothecary in many countries.

The dispensing of prescription medicine is overseen by the **Food and Drug Administration (FDA)** in the United States. The pharmacist is usually a wonderful **source** of information such as drug ingredients, drug interactions, proper dosages, side effects, and **generic equivalents**, as well as prescriptions. The **Rx** (some say *Rx* is from the Latin for recipe) is represented on labels, stores, and elsewhere.

Even for those fluent in English, drug labels and explanations can be confusing or difficult to understand. FDA regulations call for **full disclosure** of all possible side effects and drug interactions, so the language is technical.

Phrases to Say When Calling or Talking to the Pharmacy

→ What are your hours?

→ When are you open until?

→ Are you a **24-hour pharmacy**?

→ Do you accept _____ (checks, cash, credit cards, debit cards)?

→ What ID do I need? I just moved here from _____ (your country).

→ I have a prescription that I need _____ (today, tonight, in 24 hours). Will that be a problem?

→ Is there a **drive-through** at your drugstore?

→ Is there someone _____ (there, in the drugstore, in your department) who speaks _____ (your language)?

→ Is there a Language Line to translate or interpret the _____ (instructions, directions, label information) for me into my language?

→ Do you carry homeopathic remedies?

→ May I _____ (pay for, check out, purchase) other items at the pharmacy counter, or do I have to go to a separate cashier?

Doctors, hospitals, pharmacies, etc., ask for a list of medications. Make a list and keep it with you. The list should include vitamins, homeopathic remedies, and other herbal substances. This list will be used many times.

Phrases to Use in the Pharmacy

→ Are you the pharmacist?

→ May I speak with the pharmacist?

→ The/My doctor gave me this prescription.

→ I am a new customer.

→ I am _____ (new here, new in the United States).

→ Do I need to _____ (fill out a form, show you identification)?

→ May I pay with _____ (a credit card, a debit card, a check, cash)?

→ When will the prescription be ready?

→ When can I pick up the medication?

→ Do you deliver? I _____ (don't drive, don't have a car, have a vision problem, just had surgery).

→ May I _____ (wait for this, come back later, pick this up tomorrow)?

→ How long will this take?

→ How much will this cost?

→ What type of _____ (language services, translation, telephone interpretation, in-person interpretation) do you provide?

➜ I don't need a **childproof cap**. There are no children in my home, and it is too difficult for me to open, because I have _____ (arthritis, rheumatism).

➜ May I renew prescriptions over the phone?

Phrases to Use When Talking with the Pharmacist

➜ How often should I take this?

➜ How many times a day?

➜ Does this interact with my other prescriptions?

➜ Here's a **list of medications** I'm taking.

➜ Is there a generic equivalent for this drug?

➜ Is the generic as **effective** as the name brand?

➜ How much does the generic cost?

➜ What are the side effects of this prescription?

➜ Can I drive after taking this medicine?

➜ Will this make me **drowsy**?

➜ Should I take this with _____ (food, meals)?

➜ Should I take this _____ (without food, **on an empty stomach**)?

➜ Do I take this _____ (first thing in the morning, before bed)?

➜ Does this medication come in _____ (a tablet, a capsule, a liquid, a **flavored** liquid)?

→ My child can't take pills; does this come in a liquid?

→ Does this **cough** medicine come in a flavored liquid?

→ Do you have translating capability to give me instructions in my native language?

Phrases You May Hear on a Recorded Message When You Call the Pharmacy

→ This is _____ (name of store).

→ Press _____ (number on the keypad) to _____ (speak to a pharmacist, speak to the pharmacy department, **renew** your prescription, **refill** a prescription).

→ Please _____ (say, **punch in**, **press**, enter) your prescription number.

→ Please _____ (hold on, wait) while we _____ (check, confirm, look up) your prescription.

→ Press 1 to confirm a pickup time, 2 to fill another prescription.

→ Your prescription will be _____ (ready, done, filled) _____ (today, tomorrow). Press 1 to enter a pickup time.

→ We _____ (have to, must, will) check with your _____ (physician, doctor) about a _____ (renewal, refill). We'll call you _____ (about a pickup time, if there's a problem).

→ To end this call, press _____ (**star**, **pound**, 0, any key).

Phrases You May Hear from the Pharmacist

→ Do you have any questions about this drug?

→ We don't have the complete prescription.

→ May I give you these to _____ (**tide you over, hold you, keep you going**) until I _____ (order, get, find at another store) _____ (the rest, the remainder, more) of this medication?

→ Did you know that this medication comes in a generic form?

→ Did your doctor tell you that this prescription is available in a generic form?

→ The generic is available for _____ (half the price, much less, a lower cost).

Idioms and Other Vocabulary

Administer: give out

Childproof cap: bottle cap made so that children cannot open the cap (lid or top) of the container

Cough: sound of air being sent out of the throat (passage at back of mouth)

Dispensed: gave out

Drive-through (*also* **drive-thru**): place in some pharmacies, banks, or stores where you don't get out of the car but instead drive up to a window and do business

Drowsy: tired, falling asleep

Effective: working well, doing a good job

Flavored: given a better taste (In medicines, this is especially done for children.)

Food and Drug Administration (FDA): federal government agency that checks to see if food and drugs are safe

Formerly: at a time before

Full disclosure: tell everything about a subject

Generic equivalents: drugs not made by a particular pharmaceutical manufacturer and, therefore, not sold under a brand name

Hold you: provide you enough until the full prescription becomes available

Inoculations: injections to protect against particular diseases

Interchangeably: with the same meaning (For words used interchangeably, you may say or write either word.)

Interpret: change spoken language to another language

Keep you going: give you a supply until you can get more

Language Line: service that interprets or translates spoken or written language

List of medications: list of all the medicines you are taking

On an empty stomach: before eating or drinking anything

Over-the-counter: available for sale without a prescription (Over-the-counter medications are usually on shelves in the store, not behind the counter, table, or shelf that separates you from the prescription medications and the pharmacist.)

Pound: the # on a telephone

Press: push down, as a number on the telephone (The term also means to iron—pronounced /ayern/—clothes.)

Punch in: push down, as a number on the telephone

Renew (*also* **refill)**: get more of

Rx: the written abbreviation of the word *prescription*

Source: where something comes from

Star: the * on a telephone

Tide you over: provide a temporary supply that is enough to take until the full supply becomes available

Translate: change written language to another language

24-hour pharmacy: a pharmacy that never closes, is open 24 hours a day, every day

Part 2 Notes Section

_____

_____

_____

_____

_____

_____

_____

_____

_____

_____

_____

_____

_____

_____

_____

_____

_____

_____

_____

_____

PART 3

Discovering Community Resources

Active Learning Advice: Watch TV in English

Watch TV in English, even if you start with 10 minutes a day or night. If you live with your family or friends, watch 10 minutes or a short program together in English. Keep a small pad of paper and a pen or pencil nearby. Write down in English or in your language any words, situations, or ideas that you don't understand. After the program, during the commercials, or during a **pause** you **create**, you and the others can discuss your questions or other things you have written down. They may understand what you don't; you may understand what they don't. If you have recorded the program, you may watch it again after the discussion, looking up words in the dictionary or checking the new vocabulary on your computer. Regularly increase the amount of time watching/speaking in English.

Good Programs for Starting This Activity

- Children's TV programs—Cartoons, "Sesame Street," "Dora the Explorer," or whatever is popular and **appropriate**. Watch with the children in the house, with adults, or alone.

- **Soap operas**—The plots of these programs are similar to the plots of the soap operas of your native country. The characters, the settings, and the situations are **constant**. These are *not* for watching with children.

- Reality or game shows—"Dancing with the Stars," "American Idol," "The Biggest Loser," and other shows where an activity is taking place are easier to understand than quiz shows where the question-and-answer format is more difficult to **keep track of**.

- News shows are more **complex** unless you are familiar with the news (know it from news in your language). Speech is usually faster and the program moves quickly from **topic** to topic.

- Rent or buy videos or DVDs of older TV shows. The language is often easier to understand. Examples of these include "I Love Lucy," "The Mary Tyler Moore Show," "Cheers," and many other situation comedies (**sitcoms**).

- Commercials are particularly good for hearing the latest language (idioms, new computer words, and terms for the latest products). Watching them also lets you observe more about the latest cultural **trends**.

Idioms and Other Vocabulary

Appropriate: good for the situation, what is needed

Complex: difficult to understand

Constant: happening regularly

Create: make happen (For example, create time to talk by pausing the TV or saying, "Let's stop every 15 minutes to review.")

Keep track of: follow, understand

Pause: short stop before starting again

Sitcoms: short for situation comedies, funny TV programs in which the same people appear in different situations

Soap operas (*also* serials): ongoing TV programs aired in separate sections (Soap operas got this name because some operas have romantic and/or tragic plots similar to these programs and originally most of the advertisers for the programs were soap companies.)

Topic: subject

Trends: the way the culture is changing

CHAPTER 9

First Responders: Fire Departments, Police Departments, and Emergency Medical Personnel

F irst responders are people trained to be at emergencies and dangerous situations that require immediate attention. These situations include fires, crimes, and medical issues. When there is such an emergency, the telephone number to call for help is 9-1-1, which is pronounced nine-one-one, *not* nine-eleven. Call 9-1-1 only for a true emergency. It is **considered a crime** to use this telephone number for **less** serious situations.

Especially if you have children, it is a good idea to plan trips to a local fire department, police department, and hospital.

An exercise you might have with your family or group might be to come up with a list of questions to ask at these places so that you get the most information and help possible. Call first to see about the best time for your visits. Even with an appointment, these visits may be **interrupted** by an emergency the responders need to address.

The Fire Marshall's Association of North America sponsors the program **EDITH**, which means **Exit Drills in the Home**. This program **encourages** families to plan ahead.

Phrases You May Hear at Your Local Fire Department

➔ Practice; have fire drills.

➔ Do not have matches where children can get them.

➔ Don't play with matches.

➔ Don't try to put out a fire yourself.

➔ Don't fight a fire yourself.

➔ Plan a place for everyone to meet outside the house and away from the house and trees.

➔ Decide on ways to _____ (exit, leave, get out of) the home.

➔ Find exits from each room in the home; these are doors and windows.

➔ Close the door when leaving a room to try to **contain** the fire.

→ Touch the top part of a door; do not open it if it is hot.

→ Open a door slowly if it is cool and close it quickly if smoke or heat is **present**.

→ Do not use elevators; use stairs.

→ You need _____ (a smoke detector, a fire extinguisher, an **escape ladder**).

→ Make certain that children understand not to hide _____ (under furniture, in closets).

→ Get out fast.

→ Don't take time to _____ (get dressed, get your things, find your pets).

→ **Crawl** on the floor because there is more fresh air there.

→ Call 9-1-1 _____ (from a neighbor's house, using a cell phone you have with you and not one you stopped to look for) after everyone is out of the house at the meeting place.

→ Tell the emergency operator _____ (the address, the apartment number, the cross street, the telephone number you are calling from, the **type of fire**).

→ Speak slowly and clearly; answer all questions.

→ Do not keep gasoline stored in your house or garage.

→ If you have an open fireplace, use a **screen** in front of the fireplace.

→ Do not leave clothing or newspaper near a space heater or stove.

→ Don't leave cigarettes burning in ashtrays.

→ Dispose of fireplace ashes properly.

Phrases to Say at the Fire Station

→ When should people call 9-1-1 about a fire?

→ What do we say when we call about _____ (a fire, smoke)?

→ When should people just call the fire department for information?

→ What type of information?

→ What are the responsibilities of a fire fighter?

→ Where is the alarm?

→ May we see the **hook and ladder**?

→ How many smoke alarms should we have in our _____ (house, home, apartment, condo), and where should they be?

→ What kind of fire alarm do we need? Is one alarm enough?

→ We like to light candles at dinner. Is that OK?

→ What if the electricity goes out?

→ My daughter talks about becoming a fire fighter. What are the _____ (requirements, skills, classes) she should know about?

Phrases You May Hear at the Police Station

→ You may call the local police station for town or city emergencies.

→ You may call the local police about local directions.

→ Call 9-1-1 about crimes such as _____ (breaking and entering, robbery, burglary, stolen cars, vandalism).

→ Drivers should **obey** speed limits and traffic rules.

→ You may get tickets and points on your license for speeding and other **infractions** of the law.

→ You may also have your driver's license **suspended** or **revoked**.

→ Check with the **DMV** about the rules in your state.

→ Trim bushes that block the view from windows or make hiding places.

→ Trim trees that provide **access** to a second-floor window.

→ Don't open your door to strangers.

→ Make sure all windows and all outside doors can be **securely** locked.

→ Make sure all fences and gates lock securely and that they are strong.

→ If you have a garage, keep it locked.

→ Use outside lighting for evenings and an **automatic timer** to turn lights on and off for sunup and sundown and when you are away.

→ Use a safe-deposit box at your bank or a vault with a dead-lock at home for your most valuable property and papers.

→ List identifying numbers, serial and otherwise, and pictures of jewelry and artifacts in a safe place to identify objects that may be **fenced**.

Phrases to Say at the Police Station

→ What does the chief of police do?

→ What does a detective do?

→ What does a police officer do?

→ What is a _____ (cop, **plainclothes officer**, traffic policeman, police commissioner)?

→ When should we call 9-1-1?

→ When should we call the police station for information?

→ Is the jail in the police station?

→ May we see your badge, and could you explain what everything on it means?

→ Someone stole my bike from school last week. I reported it to the school; should I _____ (report it to you, fill out a report)?

→ I saw _____ (someone, a suspect) riding a bicycle like mine that day.

→ I think I can _____ (describe, tell you) what he looks like.

→ My friend was with me; he was a witness.

→ My son thinks he would like to be a police officer. What does he need to do? What courses does he need to take, and what training should he have?

It would be difficult to interview a **paramedic** or an **EMT** unless you were in an emergency situation yourself. It is a **growing field** of work and a lot of training is involved. Certain

personality traits, **physical characteristics**, and **family conditions** would help you to follow this route. There is much information about the field on the Internet. If you need more, you could ask at a local hospital for more information.

Phrases You May Hear When Calling 9-1-1 for Crimes and Fire (Nonmedical)

→ Do you want help from the police, the fire department, or an ambulance?

→ What are you reporting?

→ Please speak in short, clear sentences.

→ I'm transferring you to someone who speaks _____ (your language).

→ I'm sending an ambulance.

→ I'm sending a fire truck.

→ I'm sending a patrol car.

→ Where is it happening?

→ Where are you now?

→ What is your (complete) name?

→ Suspect description?

→ Vehicle description?

→ Don't hang up.

→ A unit is on its way to you.

→ Do you _____ (see, smell) smoke?

→ Where's the fire?

→ How many people are in the _____ (building, home)?

→ Is there anyone inside?

→ Is anyone injured?

→ Please keep calm.

→ Help is on the way.

Idioms and Other Vocabulary

Access: way to enter

Automatic timer: a device that can be set to turn lights on and off at specific times

Considered: thought to be

Contain: keep from spreading

Crawl: go along on your hands and knees

Crime: an illegal act

Cross street: the street that meets your street at the corner and leads to and from your street

DMV: Department of Motor Vehicles

EDITH (Exit Drills in the Home): a process for planning to get your family safely out of your home if a fire starts (This plan is sponsored by the Fire Marshall's Association of North America.)

EMT: emergency medical technician, person trained to give care to people before they get to a hospital

Encourages: promotes, gets people to do

Escape ladder: a folding metal ladder that can hook onto a windowsill

Family conditions: responsibilities to your family (To be an EMT, you must be able to leave suddenly and at any time to help people.)

Fenced: sold illegally gotten or stolen goods

Growing field: type of work with more jobs becoming available

Hide: get out of sight

Hook and ladder: a fire engine with long ladders attached to it

Infractions: law-breaking or rule-breaking acts

Interrupted: stopped while still in progress

Less: not as much as, not as important as

Obey: do what you are told

Paramedic: person trained to do work of a doctor or nurse yet not one

Personality traits: character, such as sensitivity to people, caring

Physical characteristic: feature of one's body and what it can do (For example, first responders need strength, such as strong legs and a strong back for lifting people.)

Plainclothes officer: police person who doesn't wear a uniform but wears regular clothing in order to not be recognized as an officer

Present: there, in existence, visible or felt

Revoked: officially canceled

Screen: wire net inside a frame

Securely: attached tightly

Suspended: officially stopped for a period of time

Type of fire: description of where and how a fire started (for example, started in the kitchen or bedroom, started with a match, spilled gasoline, or an overturned candle)

CHAPTER 10

The Post Office

The United States Postal Service (USPS) does much more than just deliver the mail. The USPS sells stamps, postal supplies, and money orders. It also sends mail and packages, including the necessary customs forms for sending mail and packages out of the country. For U.S. citizens, it has all the necessary forms for getting or renewing a passport—and will even take a passport photo.

Additionally, the post office has an active role in community affairs such as helping to find missing children, trying to locate bone marrow donors, alerting the neighborhood about wanted criminals, and performing other valuable services.

The USPS also can help customers connect with other government agencies.

Phrases You May Hear at the Post Office

→ How may I help you?

→ Next person in line, please!

→ Is there anything _____ (**hazardous**, liquid, break-able, **fragile**) in this package?

→ Would you like to insure this?

→ Would you like to track this package?

→ Do you want delivery confirmation?

→ How quickly would you like this to arrive at the destination?

→ Do you want to send this **Media Mail**? You can do this if it is only a book or a video.

→ You forgot to put the **zip code** on this letter. Do you know it or should I look it up?

→ There is no **return address** on the upper left corner of this letter. Do you want to _____ (add it, put it on, do it and return to the window)? You don't have to wait in line again.

→ Please tape this box securely.

→ Would you like to buy stamps as well?

Phrases to Say at the Post Office: Mailing

→ When will the (letter, package) that I'm sending arrive?

→ What are my shipment choices and prices for each?

→ How much does it cost to send this package _____
(first class, two-day mail, **overnight**, media rate)?

→ I sent a _____ (letter, package) last week and it
hasn't arrived. Can you check?

→ I want to send this with _____ (**tracking**, **return
receipt**, signature request).

→ I want to send this _____ (regular mail, priority mail,
overnight).

→ May I insure this package for _____ ($50, $100, $500)?

→ Is it OK to use this box for shipping?

→ Is this envelope _____ (**too large**, **too thick**, **too
heavy**) for a first-class stamp?

→ Which is faster, Priority or Express Mail?

→ How much does it cost to send a one-ounce letter to
_____ (Ecuador, Russia, Thailand)? How much does
each additional ounce cost?

→ May I use a **Forever Stamp** on this letter to Canada?

→ How much will the postage be to send this letter to Mexico?

Phrases to Say at the Post Office: Services

→ What are your hours, and are you open on weekends?

→ Do you sell _____ (address labels, Scotch tape,
packing tape, post cards)?

→ May I have _____ (change-of-address cards, a card
to request that you hold my mail), please?

→ I'd like to buy _____ (a roll, a sheet, a book) of stamps.

→ How much does a _____ (**roll**, **sheet**, **book**) of stamps cost?

→ Can you **hold my mail** for _____ (a week, a month)?

→ I received a **notice** that you're holding a _____ (letter, package) for me.

→ I'd like to **rent a post office box**.

→ I need **change-of-address cards**, please.

→ I'd like a money order, please.

→ How much does a money order for _____ ($150, $300, $1,000) cost?

→ May I pay my electric bill here?

Idioms and Other Vocabulary

Book: *see* **Roll**

Change-of-address cards: information cards you fill out to ensure that your mail is sent to the new address when you move

Forever Stamp: USPS term for a stamp without postage printed on it that is good no matter what the current postage rate is

Fragile: delicate, easily broken

Hazardous: dangerous

Hold my mail: keep my mail at the post office when I go away, so I can pick it up there when I return

Media Mail: USPS term for a postage rate that is cheaper than regular mail but can be used only for books and videos

Notice: communication sent to you from the post office (For example, sometimes the post office sends you notices about mail it is holding for you or other postal issues.)

Overnight: mail sent one day to be received the next day

Rent a post office box: pay for the use of a storage box at the post office that may be rented for a relatively small charge (Different-size post office boxes may be rented; your mail can be sent there instead of to your home or office.)

Return address: your address in the upper left corner (If the mail you are sending doesn't arrive at the destination, this information can help the post office return it to you.)

Return receipt: receipt signed by person to whom you sent a letter or package

Roll (*or* **sheet** *or* **book) of stamps**: quantities of stamps that you may buy

Sheet: *see* **Roll**

Too large (*or* **too thick** *or* **too heavy) for a first-class stamp**: greater than the size or weight that you may mail for the price of one first-class stamp (Size or thickness may make it necessary to use additional postage.)

Tracking: following information about your mail to check the date and time it was delivered and who received it

Zip code: one of the five-digit numbers assigned to every area in the United States (The zip code helps the post office deliver the mail more easily.)

CHAPTER 11

The Bank

Banks offer checking and savings accounts as well as other **financial services**. Lending departments provide personal and business loans, mortgages, and **lines of credit**. Your banker can help you send money by **wire transfers**. Financial advice and **investment brokerage** services are available at some banks. Banks offer their own credit cards and may provide life insurance. Most banks have **branches** within communities, states, and throughout the country. Major banks are international.

Banks charge many **fees** for services. Often these charges are not clear. Ask about them. You may also be able to earn **interest** on certain accounts. Ask questions to ensure that you get all the **benefits** available to you.

Phrases You May Hear in the Bank

→ You must **maintain** a **balance** of at least $100 in your checking account to avoid fees.

→ If you maintain a balance of at least _____ ($100, $500, $1,000), we will pay you interest.

→ Your money is insured by the **Federal Deposit Insurance Corporation (FDIC)** for up to $250,000.

→ If you write a check for more than you have in your checking account, we will not **honor** it.

→ If you write a check that exceeds your balance, we will charge you a $25 fee.

→ Would you like to arrange for us to use your savings account to **cover** an **overdraft** in your checking account?

→ We provide **overdraft protection**.

→ We offer many savings choices: savings accounts, **CDs**, money market accounts, cash back on debit cards.

→ Do you have your **bank card**?

→ May I see your ID?

→ Do you know how to use the **ATM**?

→ Some companies, such as _____ (utilities, mortgage companies, cell phone providers), may, with your written consent, automatically charge your checking account. Know which these are so you can deduct those charges from your balance.

Phrases to Say in the Bank

→ I want to open a savings account.

→ I want to open a checking account.

→ How much must I keep in my checking account to earn interest?

→ What is your current interest rate on savings accounts?

→ Please explain your **debit card** program.

→ What fees should I expect? Please explain.

→ Can you show me how to use the ATM?

→ How do I manage my account online?

→ I would like to pay my bills online. Can you help me with that?

→ I'd like to talk with someone about a _____ (personal loan, business loan, **home equity loan**).

→ I would like to learn about _____ (getting a mortgage, **refinancing** a mortgage).

→ My _____ (husband, wife, partner) and I want to open a **joint** _____ (savings, checking) account.

→ I would like to add my _____ (husband, wife, part-ner, son, daughter) to my _____ (savings account, checking account, CD, money market account).

→ How do I open an account for my newborn granddaughter?

→ I have a small business in town, and I would like a line of credit to help me _____ (manage **cash flow**, buy equipment, expand my staff).

→ My check was returned by the telephone company. Why?

→ How can I prevent this from happening in the future?

→ May I have a money order for _____ (amount)?

→ Can you help me wire money to my son in _____ (California, India)?

→ I hear that you offer a _____ (Christmas Club, Holiday Club) account. Please explain how that works.

Idioms and Other Vocabulary

ATM: automatic teller machine, a machine that will cash your checks, take your deposits, and allow your withdrawals without a human teller

Balance: the amount of money in your account at all times

Bank card: a bank customer card that proves identification to protect the customer and the bank

Benefits: things that are in your favor or best interest

Branches (*also* stores): bank locations

Cash flow: movement of money in and out of business or personal accounts

CDs: certificates of deposit that have a stated maturity date and interest rate

Cover: make up the amount of money you are short

Debit card: card that permits an immediate deduction from your bank account for a charge

Federal Deposit Insurance Corporation (FDIC): the department of the U.S. government that insures all banks and their deposits up to $250,000 per person

Fees: money charged for services

Financial services: any service that helps you manage your money

Home equity loan: money borrowed by using home ownership as security

Honor: allow, cash

Interest: money your money earns

Investment brokerage: a service that invests clients' money for them in stocks and bonds for a fee

Joint: involving two or more people

Lines of credit: access to borrowing money from banks or other lending institutions

Maintain: keep

Overdraft: writing a check for more money than you have in your account

Overdraft protection: a service that the bank offers to honor checks that are overdrawn and treat the money as a loan with interest

Refinancing: money provided again for a large purchase, maybe a home, to improve the terms of the original loan

Wire transfers: a way to send money from one bank to another without physically sending a check

CHAPTER 12

The Library

The local public library used to be a place that **loaned** books to adults and children and offered **occasional** lectures and **story hours**. Today's libraries often provide so many services that they **function** as community centers. Not only are libraries the **sites** for **unlimited** services, programs, and materials, but **librarians** and others who work in libraries are **highly trained**. They are helpful and knowledgeable about what their library offers and where to start looking for whatever you may need to know. The local public library is a wonderful place to start your search for help in many areas.

Libraries offer lectures on numerous topics, book signings for local authors and others, **self-help** programs and activities, and a **broad array** of children's programs. Additionally, they may **partner with** other community organizations to bring concerts and other cultural activities to the area.

Phrases You May Hear at the Library

→ May I help you?

→ Would you like a library card?

→ In addition to your library card application, we need a current driver's license.

→ You can search for titles using this online catalog.

→ This book is **overdue**.

→ The **fine** is _____ (50¢, $1.25, amount).

→ We don't have that book right now.

→ Would you like to be on the waiting list for that book?

→ This is a **reference book**. You may read it here but cannot **check it out**.

→ We can get a book from any library in _____ (the system, the county, the state).

→ Do you want us to check which library might have the book you want and _____ (order it, get it, have it sent here) for you?

→ Do you need help with _____ (the computer, the copy machine)?

→ The **restrooms** are located on the second floor.

→ I can help you find _____ (the **large-print book** section, the CD collection, our DVD shelves, today's lecture room).

→ Are you on our mailing list?

Phrases You May Hear at the Library: Disciplinary

➜ Please _____ (be quiet, keep your voice down).

➜ Please turn off your cell phone.

➜ I'm sorry; this is a no-smoking building.

➜ Please, no food or drink is allowed in the library.

Phrases to Say at the Library: General Services

➜ I'd like to get a library card.

➜ What are your hours?

➜ Are you closed on _____ (name of a holiday, Sundays, weekends)?

➜ I live at _____ (your address). Do you have a **branch** closer to my home?

➜ How can I receive your newsletter?

➜ Do you have a website?

➜ When are these books **due**?

➜ May I just return these books in the **book drop**? They are not overdue.

➜ This book was due last week. What is the fine?

➜ Do you have _____ (title of a book)?

➜ Do you have a **waiting list** for that book?

→ Where are the _____ (cookbooks, travel books, large-print books, nonfiction books, **foreign-language books**, novels, children's books)?

→ Do have _____ (yesterday's newspaper, the *Philadelphia Inquirer*)?

→ Do have magazines? Where?

→ Do you have **audiobooks**?

→ Do you have a **book club**?

→ How do I check out an **e-book**?

→ Do you have books in foreign languages?

→ Do you have books about starting a small business?

→ May I take one of these library maps?

→ Do you have a photocopier?

> Many people like to listen to audiobooks while they drive or do housework. People with vision or eye problems also listen to audiobooks.

Phrases to Say at the Library: Digital Services

→ I would like to use a computer. Is there a charge for this?

→ How long may I stay on the computer?

→ Can I print from this computer? Is there a charge for printing?

→ Do you have Wi-Fi so I can use my laptop?

→ Do you offer computer classes? When? What do they cost?

Phrases to Say at the Library: Special Programs

→ I read about children's programs. Can you tell me more?

→ When are the children's story hours?

→ Do you have a summer reading program for children?

→ I'm interested in my family history. Do you have a genealogy section?

→ Do you offer _____ (English classes, English conversation classes, **ESL**, **ESOL**, **citizenship classes**)? What do they cost?

→ May I have a schedule for (**book signings**, readings, lectures)?

→ Can you tell me where I can (**register to vote**, get an **absentee ballot**, pay my taxes)?

→ Where do I sign up for _____ (ESL classes, the business series, the children's program)?

→ Is there a fee for that?

→ Do you offer business classes? Can you tell me where else I might find them?

→ Do you provide help with **résumé** writing?

→ If I attend a lecture, do you offer _____ (**babysitting**, child care)?

Idioms and Other Vocabulary

Absentee ballot: system where people can mail in their vote because they will be away when voting takes place where they vote

Audiobooks: books that you can listen to from recordings on cassette tapes or CDs

Babysitting: service in which qualified people are hired to care for children while their parents are attending library programs

Book club: group where people read the same book or author and meet to discuss what they have read

Book drop: place to return books that are on time, not overdue

Book signings: events at which authors autograph or sign books for sale that they have written

Branch: location, some libraries have several branches

Broad array: a wide range, many choices.

Check it out (*also* **take it out**): remove from the library, with permission, to read and then return to the library

Citizenship classes: classes to help people prepare to take the citizenship test

Due: the date when the book must be returned to the library

E-book: book in a digital format (nonpaper)

ESL, ESOL: English as a Second Language, English for Speakers of Other Languages

Fine: A small amount of money, usually figured out by each day late, that you pay to the library when you don't return a book on time.

Foreign-language books: books printed in your language or another language other than English (In addition to reading in English, which you are learning, you may need or want to read something in your language.)

Function: work as

Highly trained: trained carefully for the work they do

Large-print book: book printed in larger than usual type (These books are easier to read for older people and people with vision problems.)

Librarians: people who have studied and have degrees in library science

Loan (*also* **lend**): give someone a book or other library media that must be returned

Occasional: happening or occurring sometimes

Overdue: late, after the time it should be returned

Partner with: join with, do together with

Reference book: book with specific information needed for many people to use at the library (Examples are a book of maps [atlas], a dictionary, and an encyclopedia.)

Register to vote: sign up to vote in elections

Restrooms: bathrooms, men's and ladies' rooms (The word *toilets* is used for these rooms in many countries but is not accepted as a polite way to say it in the United States.)

Résumé: a written description of educational and work experience used when applying for work

Self-help: materials to help or learn by yourself, on your own, without a teacher or a class

Sites: locations where something happened or is happening

Story hours: programs for young children in which a library employee reads stories to groups of children

Unlimited: without a set beginning or end

Waiting list: a list of names of people who want a book that is unavailable because someone has checked it out of the library (If you are on a waiting list, the library will call you or send you an e-mail when the book becomes available.)

Part 3 Notes Section

_____

_____

_____

_____

_____

_____

_____

_____

_____

_____

_____

_____

_____

_____

_____

_____

_____

_____

_____

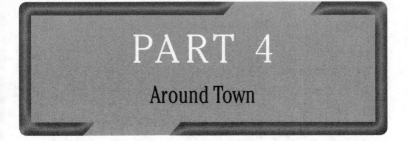

PART 4

Around Town

Active Learning Advice: Speak English in One Room

Speak English with family or friends when you are in one **particular** room. For example, "Every time we are in the kitchen, we'll speak English." You can even write words in English on **Post-it Notes** and put the notes on appliances, furniture, objects, and even food. You may also write English pronunciation hints on the Post-it Notes. Every time you open the refrigerator, say "refrigerator"; every time you have a glass of milk, say "glass" and "milk."

At first it will be a relief to finish eating and leave the kitchen, but it will become easier and even fun. After several weeks, change rooms or add another room to **label** and in which to speak English. Keep doing the exercise in two rooms; don't **eliminate** the first room. You will learn a lot of English vocabulary and have a good time. Check vocabulary pronunciation with a friend, a **colleague**, or on the computer.

After you **master** the words, you may say **relevant** sentences:

→ **Pass** the _____ (salt, pepper, milk, butter, rice, vegetables), please.

→ I really like _____ (the chicken, the dessert, the new kitchen table).

Culture Hints

Many ESL students confuse the pronunciation of *kitchen* and *chicken*. They may say, "I'm cooking dinner in the chicken."

Dessert is a word that is easy to confuse with similar English words:

dessert (*n*): a treat after a meal   /dezért/

desert (*n*): dry arid land   /dézert/

desert (*v*) abandon, leave   /dezért/

We ate our *dessert* in the *desert* before we had to *desert* the *desert*.

Idioms and Other Vocabulary

Colleague: person who works with you

Eliminate: take away

Label: put a note with information on something (objects in the room)

Master: be excellent at

Particular: special

Pass: give to another person

Post-it Notes: trademark name for a pad of sticky paper, used for notes

Relevant: having to do with a subject

CHAPTER 13

Getting Around:
Asking Directions and Parking

The chapters in Part 4 focus on the kinds of tasks and situations you'll find as you move about your community, but first this chapter looks at simple logistics: finding your way and then parking.

In the United States, people are generally eager to help with advice, directions, and problem solving. People in this country are also usually patient when trying to understand and help someone whose first language is not English. Sometimes they offer help if you are standing on a street corner looking lost and in need of directions. Most of the time, however, you have to ask for the advice or help you need. In large major cities, people are often more rushed and may not have the time to discuss in detail the answers to your questions, so be prepared to look further for someone who is more available.

Phrases to Get Started Asking for Information

→ Excuse me . . .

→ Pardon me . . .

→ May I interrupt you?

→ Please, can you help me?

→ I am new to this area.

→ I am lost.

→ I'm a little turned around.

Many public facilities, shops, and companies will list directions on their own websites, so before planning a trip, take a quick check for this service. Usually, these sources provide the best directions. Other websites offering maps and general directions aren't always up-to-date on road closures or traffic changes. Bus, train, and other public transportation systems offer directions and schedules—often available at their websites for download. However, sometimes these change frequently, so make sure you have the latest information.

A vehicle is necessary to get around in most areas of the United States. Large cities such as New York or Chicago may be exceptions because there are many **modes** of public transportation available: train, subway, bus, taxicab, and, of course, walking. If you choose to use a car, you may, of course, buy, lease, and even rent for a day.

Reminder: Before you drive in the United States, familiarize yourself with the traffic signs and lights, because they may differ from those in your country. Driving rules differ from state to state in the United States, so make sure you know them as well.

Phrases for Asking Directions

→ I am lost. Could you give me directions?

→ I am confused. Do you know the way to _____ (destination)?

→ Could you help me with directions? I need to get to _____ (destination).

→ I think I made a wrong turn somewhere.

→ Where is the highway entrance ramp?

→ Can you tell me where _____ (destination) is?

→ Do you know where _____ (destination) is?

→ Where is _____ (destination)?

→ Can you direct me to the nearest gas station? I _____ (am low on gas, need air in my tires).

→ Which way is the bus/train station?

→ I am trying to get to _____ (destination). Can you help me?

→ How do I get to _____ (destination)?

→ Where can I find a **convenience store**?

→ I am looking for a _____ (Chinese, Japanese, Greek, Spanish, French, Italian, typical American, fast-food, take-out, vegetarian, inexpensive) restaurant.

→ Is there a cash machine nearby?

→ I am trying to find the post office. Could you please tell me where it is?

→ What is the _____ (easiest, best, most direct, shortest, fastest) way to get to _____ (destination)?

→ I'm lost! Can you please show me where the _____ (elevators, escalators) are?

→ Is Dr. Smith in this building?

→ Are there restrooms on this floor?

→ Can you direct me to the _____ (men's, women's) restrooms?

→ Thank you for your help.

→ I appreciate your help.

Parking Downtown

You'll find that the annoyance of finding parking in busy cities is the subject of much U.S. small talk!

Phrases for Parking Situations

→ Where is a _____ (parking lot, parking garage)?

→ Is there a parking garage near here?

→ May I park on the street?

→ Is this free parking?

→ Can I park here overnight, or does this garage close and at what time?

→ This parking meter is broken. Will I get a ticket or get **towed**?

→ Excuse me. Do you have to pay for parking on Sundays?

→ Do you have change for a dollar?

→ Do you have quarters for the meter?

→ Where is the **pay machine**?

→ Do I need to get my ticket **validated**?

Idioms and Other Vocabulary

Convenience store: store that is easy to get to and sells food and other products that may be needed quickly, often part of a gas station

Modes: ways or manners of travel

Pay machine: a machine used for street or parking lot payment

Towed: pulled away from an illegal parking spot by a truck used for this purpose

Validated: stamped, in the store where you have been, for free parking

CHAPTER 14

Gas and Service Stations

G as stations and service stations provide **unrelated** services in many states. This chapter offers perfect phrases related to these stations.

Gas Stations

Gas stations provide gasoline. In two states in the **contiguous** United States, New Jersey and Oregon, it is **illegal** to fill up your own gas tank. You must wait for an attendant to help you. In other states, there is **self-service** gasoline **dispensing**; you pay for the gas you want inside a **convenience store** on the **premises**, and then an attendant pushes a button to open the tank for you to help yourself to the gasoline. There is also the option to pay at the pump with a credit or debit card. Some stations may offer assistance in pumping the gas for a **fee**.

Most stations also provide a hose for you to use for putting air in your tires, if you have to use this. To use the air **dispenser**, you need to **deposit** coins into it.

Negative Prefixes

A good way to improve vocabulary is to learn *affixes*. Affixes are groups of letters added to the beginnings or ends of words to change their meanings. One type of affix is the *prefix*.

Prefixes, which are added to the beginning of a word, can change that word's meaning. Some prefixes, in fact, change a word to a completely opposite—or negative—meaning. For example *il-* before *legal* makes *legal* into *illegal*, meaning not legal. *Un-* attached to the beginning of *related* makes *unrelated*, meaning not related. Here are some examples of words with negative prefixes:

Illegible means difficult to read; *legible* is easily read.

Illiterate describes someone who has not learned to read and write; *literate* is able to read and write.

Unable means not able to do something; *able* is capable of doing something.

Unaccustomed means not used to, not familiar with; *accustomed* means the opposite.

Other negative prefixes include *in-* (*incorrect* means not correct), *dis-* (*dishonest* means not honest), *im-* (*immature* means not mature), *ir-* (*irregular* means not regular), and *non-* (*nonrefundable* means cannot be returned to get one's money back).

Suffixes are added at the ends of words to change the meanings of these words. Examples of suffixes are -*less* and -*ful*. They can change the word *care* (to think something or someone is important enough to pay attention to it or them): *careful* means trying hard to avoid doing something wrong or dangerous, and *careless* means not paying enough attention to avoid doing something wrong or dangerous.

Phrases to Use at a Gas Station

→ Fill it up.

→ **Fill 'er up** with _____ (super, regular, premium, diesel), please.

→ I'd like _____ ($10, $20, a full tank) of _____ (super, regular, premium, diesel), please.

→ What _____ (credit, debit) cards do you accept?

→ Do you take _____ (MasterCard, Visa, American Express, traveler's checks)?

→ May I pay with _____ (cash, charge card, debit card, traveler's checks)?

→ Is it _____ (cheaper, less per gallon) if I pay cash?

→ How much is (super, regular, premium, diesel) if I pay cash?

→ Is this a self-service station?

→ Do you **provide refueling** assistance?

→ Where do I pay for the gas?

➜ Do you have a _____ (restroom, ladies' room, men's room, bathroom, lavatory) available?

➜ I also want to buy a few things in the convenience store. Should I do that before or after I get the gas?

➜ I need some things in the store. May I _____ (pay for them at the same time I pay for the gas, use my credit card for both transactions)?

➜ I need some air in my tires. Where is the dispenser?

➜ How much is the air?

➜ Can you give me _____ (some change, change for a dollar)?

Service Stations

A service station is where you would take your vehicle for regular servicing like an oil change or a wide range of repairs from the simple to the more complex. Service stations may be operated **in conjunction with** gas stations or as separate **entities**.

Some stations are licensed to issue **valid state inspection stickers** after performing an inspection. They charge for this service, even though the **DMV** (Department of Motor Vehicles) performs inspections for free. Although DMV is the term used in many states, other terms for this state-run department may be used in other states.

People sometimes prefer to pay and have the inspection done at the service station, because often there are long lines and waits at the DMV for this service. A service station may conduct the inspection by appointment or, if employees aren't busy, **on the spot**. A valid inspection sticker on a car's windshield, or some other form of documentation, is necessary to avoid being in violation of the law. Each state can supply you with safety and **emission** standards needed to pass inspection.

Phrases You May Hear at a Service Station

→ Do you need _____ (a **tune-up**, an oil change)?

→ Your oil is low.

→ You need a new _____ (**oil filter**, **air filter**).

→ Check the tires?

→ Check the transmission fluid?

→ One of your headlights is out.

→ The mechanic can explain this to you.

→ Your left front tire is low.

→ Yes, we can patch tires.

Phrases to Use at a Service Station

→ Can you check out my car? The _____ (engine, starter, brake, **windshield** wipers) sound(s) strange.

→ I hear knocking in the engine.

→ What is the problem with my car?

→ Does the right rear tire look low to you?

→ I need _____ (an oil change, new tires, an inspection).

→ When can I bring the car in?

➔ Do I need to make an appointment?

➔ _____ (Should, May) I wait for my car?

➔ How long do you think I'll have to wait?

➔ Can you inspect the car and **issue** the documentation while I wait?

➔ When can I _____ (return for, pick up, come back for) my car?

➔ Can you give me _____ (an **estimate**, a written estimate) for the repair?

➔ My insurance company wants the estimate in writing.

➔ Will you accept my automobile insurance?

➔ Do you provide **loaner cars**?

➔ Is there a **warranty** for _____ (parts, service)?

➔ How long is the warranty for?

Other Auto Resources

Other automobile **venues** are **body shops**. If your car has been in an accident, you will have to go to or may be **towed** to a body shop. For this, you need to involve your insurance company. Automobile insurance coverage is necessary in the United States. Towing is usually covered by this insurance. Your insurance agent can be helpful in these situations.

There are many specialist car businesses that offer **lube jobs**, brake repair or replacement, and transmission work. Some are expert at patching tires or selling new and used tires.

There are also car washes. You may take your car to an area where there is equipment to wash and clean your own car. Other choices include car washes where you sit in your car as it is automatically moved along the cycle through wash, rinse, and air-dry. At another kind of car wash, the car is automatically moved through the cycle without anyone in the car. Both kinds of automatic car washes usually include hand-drying of the car by attendants when the car exits the cycle. Car wash choices include full service (cleaning the exterior and interior), only exterior cleaning, and **waxing**.

Idioms and Other Vocabulary

Air filter: car part that removes insects and particles so they don't reach the engine

Body shops: places where the main structure of an automobile is repaired

Contiguous: connected (The contiguous states are not separated by water or another country.)

Convenience store: store that is easy to get to and sells food and other products that may be needed quickly, often part of a gas station

Deposit: put in or into

Dispenser: machine that provides a product

Dispensing: giving out a product

DMV: Department of Motor Vehicles, state department (in some states) that handles driver's licenses, automobile registrations, and automobile inspections

Emission: a gas or other substance sent into the air, in this case by car engines

Entities: separate units

Estimate: what a company figures a cost to be

Fee: amount of money required

Fill 'er up: reduced speech for *fill her up*, fill up the gas tank (People say "her" because cars are considered female.)

Illegal: not lawful

In conjunction with: together with

Issue: give out

Loaner cars: cars that a place gives you to drive while workers repair your car

Lube jobs: services to lubricate (oil) parts of a car's engine

Oil filter: part that prevents the oil in the car from getting dirty

On the spot: not planned, immediately

Premises: land nearby

Provide: give, offer

Refueling: putting gasoline into a gas tank

Self-service: doing it yourself without help

State inspection stickers: sticker required by some states to show that a car has passed the required inspection (stickers are pieces of paper with writing on them made to attach, with adhesive, to a car's windshield)

Towed: pulled by a truck when not able to be driven

Tune-up: check of the car's engine and whatever repairs are needed for the car to run better

Unrelated: not connected

Valid: legal

Venues: places where events happen

Warranty: written promise to replace or repair something that is not as it should be

Waxing: adding a layer of wax on a car after washing it

Windshield: front window on a vehicle

CHAPTER 15

The Supermarket

n the United States, most people buy food and other **household items** in a **supermarket**. Also, some city neighborhoods have mini markets and **ethnic** markets. Many convenience stores—for example, Wawa, 7-Eleven, and Quick Chek—offer food items. These are for convenience and may cost more money. They are for last-minute purchases or emergencies.

You may hear people refer to a supermarket as the market, the grocery store, or the food market. When people are going to buy food, they may say they are going food shopping, to buy groceries, or to the market. In the United States, supermarkets are self-service with special areas within them that offer meats, fish and shellfish, deli items, and bakery items. In these areas, employees may serve you by describing items and ingredients, slicing, weighing, wrapping, packaging, and providing special food requests you may have. They may also offer free tastings of new food products. Listen to the **speaker system** for specials, tastings, and other store announcements.

Phrases You May Hear at the Supermarket

➜ May I help you?

➜ May I help you find something?

➜ Today's **specials** are _____ (two products for the price of one, buy one get one free, $1.99 today only).

➜ Watch your step. There's a spill in this aisle.

➜ Aisle 4 is closed briefly while we clear up a breakage.

➜ You can find that in aisle 4.

➜ You'll find coffee in aisle 10.

➜ Would you like to try this new sauce?

➜ No, we do not sell liquor in supermarkets in this state.

➜ I'm sorry. I don't work here. I'm just **stocking** the shelves with my company's product.

Phrases You May Hear at Checkout

➜ Will that be cash or charge?

➜ Debit or credit card?

➜ **Paper or plastic?**

→ Do you want to donate _____ ($1, $2, $3) to
   _____ (the local food bank, the American Heart
   Association, the **ASPCA**, **MADD**)?

→ Do you have any **coupons**?

→ Do you have a store card?

→ We deduct 5 cents from your total for every recyclable bag
   you bring and use.

→ Here's your receipt.

→ Save your receipts. Once you've spent _____ ($100,
   $200), you may have a free turkey for the holiday.

→ Once you've spent _____ ($50, $100, $200), you'll
   earn a _____ ($10 gift card, discount on your next
   purchase).

→ May I bring your bags to your car? No, there is no charge.
   (Note: **Tips** may be welcome.)

→ Thank you.

→ Have a nice day.

→ Do you have a receipt? If you want to return this, we need
   a receipt.

Phrases to Use at the Supermarket

→ Where can I find a shopping cart?

→ Are there any more carts with child seats?

→ There aren't any more shopping carts _____ (outside,
   in the parking lot, in here).

→ Where is the _____ (**food court**, **salad bar**, **deli** department)?

→ Can you direct me to the _____ (dairy, meat, produce, bakery, laundry detergents, coffee, deli, frozen foods) section?

→ I don't see any _____ (**extra-lean** beef, skinless chicken breasts, dark-meat chicken, meat for roasting) in the meat case.

→ Could you please **trim** the fat off of this cut of meat?

→ Do you carry **wild salmon** or only **farmed salmon**?

→ I'm looking for _____ (whole wheat pasta, cereal, chips, frozen dinners, salsa). Can you help me?

→ Do you have an **organic produce** section?

→ Do you have _____ (dairy-free, gluten-free, wheat-free) _____ (bread, crackers, pasta, desserts)?

→ Where are the fresh flowers?

→ Excuse me. I can't seem to find _____ (cut fruit, packaged salad, low-fat popcorn).

Phrases to Use at the Supermarket: Problems

→ All of the _____ (milk, cheese, yogurt, salad) of this brand expires tomorrow. Don't you have anything with a later **expiration** date?

→ You advertised that this product is on sale, but I cannot find it.

→ Are you sold out of this week's special?

→ If it's **out of stock**, do you **substitute** another?

→ Last month I bought soy chocolate pudding. I cannot find it today. Did you stop **carrying** it?

→ Where can I return this item? The can is **dented**.

→ This package was already opened.

→ When I opened the package, the _____ (cheese, yogurt, milk) was **spoiled**. I'd like a refund or a fresh product, please.

→ Excuse me. The box of _____ (**tissues**, cereal, pasta) that I want is too high. Could you please get it down for me?

Phrases to Use at the Supermarket: Other Services

→ Where is the manager's office?

→ Where is the **courtesy counter**?

→ Do you sell stamps?

→ How do I get a store card?

→ Is there a _____ (bank, ATM, eating area, **food court**) in this store?

→ Where is your **pharmacy**?

→ I'd like to pick up this prescription when I'm **through** shopping in about 30 minutes. Is that **OK**?

→ Where are the _____ (restrooms, bathrooms)? (Don't say "toilets.")

→ Where is the ladies' room?

→ Do you have a recycling center?

→ I heard that this market offers cooking classes. Where can I learn more?

→ Do you carry _____ (vitamins, beach toys, beach chairs, gloves)?

→ Can you direct me to _____ (socks, pantyhose, headbands, cotton balls)?

Phrases to Use at the Supermarket: Checking Out

→ Do you accept coupons?

→ Do you accept _____ (this discount card, personal checks, traveler's checks)?

→ I forgot my store card. I'll give you my phone number.

→ _____ (Paper, Plastic), please.

→ I have my own bags.

→ Please don't make the bags too heavy; I have to carry them upstairs.

→ Excuse me. May I get _____ (through, past you, in front of you), please? I only want to add this one item to my wife's order; she is in front of you.

→ You only have a few items; you may go ahead of me in line.

→ The express lane is closed. Do you mind if I go before you with just this one item?

→ Thank you.

Idioms and Other Vocabulary

ASPCA: American Society for the Prevention of Cruelty to Animals

Carrying: keeping in stock in the store

Coupons: special offers found in newspapers or given out by the stores

Courtesy counter: counter where customers go for service

Deli (informal for delicatessen): place in a supermarket where prepared foods and salads, cheese, cooked meats, and other items are sold by weight

Dented: bent in

Ethnic: relating to a certain race or nation

Expiration: time after which food is no longer fresh

Extra-lean: having most or all of the fat cut off

Farmed salmon (*also* farm-raised salmon): salmon that swam in contained pools

Food court: booths with different foods sold near tables and chairs at which to eat

Household items: items used within the home such as paper products and cleaning supplies

MADD: Mothers Against Drunk Driving

OK: acceptable

Organic produce: fruits and vegetables grown without the use of pesticides, grown naturally

Out of stock: not in the store

Paper or plastic?: Do you want a plastic bag or paper sack for your groceries?

Pharmacy (*also* **drugstore**): place to buy prescription drugs

Salad bar: place where you may make your own salad with cut vegetables and other items

Speaker system: electronic announcement system

Specials: good deals

Spoiled: ruined, not good to eat

Stocking: putting on the shelves

Substitute: put in place of

Supermarket: large store that sells food and many other products

Through: finished (The term also has other meanings, such as going from one end to another.)

Tips: gratuities, money given in appreciation of service

Tissues: paper products often referred to by one brand name, Kleenex

Trim: cut off, get rid of

Wild salmon: salmon that swam freely in the ocean

CHAPTER 16

Shopping, Personal Services, and Entertainment

When you resettle into a new country, there are needs that must have immediate attention. Food, clothing, personal and health needs all fall into that category. Most of those immediate needs have been covered in the previous chapters. This chapter offers perfect phrases for less-urgent, more-everyday needs, such as shopping in a department store, getting your hair cut, or finding a dry cleaner.

Phrases for Shopping in a Department Store

→ Where can I find women's shoes?

→ Do you carry _____ (cosmetics, children's games, greeting cards, **cookware**, **jewelry**)?

→ I'm traveling out of the country. Do you have a luggage department?

→ Where are the _____ (**dressing rooms**, **fitting rooms**)?

→ I would like to see this dress in a size 10.

→ My husband prefers polo shirts.

→ May I return this if it doesn't fit?

→ What is your warranty policy?

→ This was on the sale rack, but it isn't marked down. Could you **scan it**, please?

→ No one is at the cash register in Boys' Clothes. May I _____ (buy, pay for, check out) these at your register?

→ Are these coupons still valid?

→ I've had this gift card for more than a year. May I still use it?

→ I was told I needed to check with Customer Service; where is it?

→ I would like to return these shoes. Here is my receipt.

→ Can you direct me to the _____ (elevator, escalator)?

→ Is there a gift-wrapping section?

→ Does this store have a restaurant, or do I have to go out and find a **freestanding** one in the _____ (mall, **strip mall**, shopping center)?

→ Which exit leads to the mall?

Phrases for Ordering Take-Out Food

→ Hello. Is this _____ (name of restaurant)?

→ I'd like an order **to go**.

→ Yes, I'd like it delivered.

→ I'll pick it up.

→ When will it be ready?

→ Please put the salad dressing **on the side**.

→ Please include plastic **utensils** and straws.

→ Do you sell _____ (soda, iced tea, bottled water)?

→ May I add the tip to my credit card now?

→ Is there a delivery charge?

Phrases for Going to the Dry Cleaner

→ What time do you close?

→ What time do you open?

→ What are your hours?

→ May I have these clothes back _____ (tomorrow, in two days, Thursday)?

→ I'd like this _____ (dress, skirt, jacket, suit) **pressed only**.

→ I'd like these shirts on hangers, please.

→ **No starch**, please.

→ Do you offer pickup and delivery service?

→ I'm sorry. This _____ (pair of pants, sweater, jacket, dress) still has a _____ (spot, stain). Can you get it out?

→ Do you launder _____ (quilts, tablecloths)?

→ What would you charge to **store** our winter coats?

→ Do you clean _____ (leather, suede, fur, wedding dresses)?

→ Oh, so where do you suggest I take it?

→ Do you have someone who does alterations?

→ I'd like to re-hem these slacks.

→ I'd like this skirt taken in.

→ This shirt needs new buttons sewn on.

Phrases for Visiting the Beauty Parlor, Beauty Salon, or Hair Salon

→ Do you take **walk-ins**?

→ What do you charge for a _____ (haircut, one-process color, manicure, pedicure)?

→ I'd like an appointment for _____ (a wash and blow-dry, a trim).

→ I have very _____ (curly, wiry, straight, unmanageable, thick) hair.

→ What product do you suggest for dry hair?

→ May I have a _____ (towel, pillow) under my neck when you shampoo my hair?

➜ Please don't blow-dry my hair. I like to **air-dry**.

➜ Can you take a little more off the _____ (sides, back)?

➜ Can you match my color?

➜ Please don't make it red.

➜ Do you use natural coloring?

➜ I'd like highlights.

➜ Do you take personal checks?

➜ May I pay with my credit card and add an amount for **cash back** for a tip?

➜ How long does a pedicure take?

➜ Do you have a mini pedicure?

➜ What are the new colors this season for manicures?

➜ Just a clear coat, please.

Phrases for Visiting a Barber Shop

➜ How long is the wait?

➜ Do you make appointments?

➜ I just want a **trim**.

➜ I like my **sideburns** _____ (long, short) and _____ (above, in the middle of, below) my ear.

➜ Can you take a little off the _____ (top, back, sides)?

➜ Do you dye hair here?

➜ I part my hair on _____ (the left, the right).

➜ I prefer to have my hair brushed back.

→ I'd like my _____ (**beard**, **moustache**, sideburns) trimmed.

→ Please don't use hair spray.

→ Thanks, but I would rather not have after-shave lotion.

→ Do you offer manicures?

→ Can I get a shave here? I don't like my razor, and the scissors I packed aren't good.

→ Do you do children's hair?

Entertainment

You may want to add some entertainment to your schedule. This can be anything from a playground to the opera. The Internet, a local telephone book, a travel guidebook for your area, and recommendations help. Also, don't forget the public library in the neighborhood where you are living. The librarian can direct you to local newspapers that tell of events and list telephone numbers to get additional information. There are many groups that are dedicated to specific interests such as music clubs, book clubs, and organizations for every hobby or interest imaginable. Share your thoughts with the librarian; he or she will be able to direct you to what you want.

Phrases for Going to the Movies

→ Are the **matinees** less expensive, or only the earliest matinee?

→ How much is a _____ (senior, student) ticket?

→ Do you have handicapped seating?

→ Where are the restrooms?

→ Excuse me. There _____ (are no paper towels, is no toilet paper) in the ladies' room.

→ How much is the _____ (popcorn, small soda, candy bar, water)?

→ Does this movie theater serve pizza and hot dogs or just popcorn, candy, and drinks?

→ I dropped my cell phone on the floor during the movie. Can you help me find it?

→ Excuse me. Would you mind moving over one seat so that my _____ (husband, friend, child) and I can sit together?

Idioms and Other Vocabulary

Air-dry: let the air dry it

Beard: facial hair on the chin

Cash back: money returned to you as cash when the cashier charges more on your credit card than the amount of your purchase

Cookware: pots and pans for cooking

Dressing rooms (*or* fitting rooms): area in a store where you can put on clothes to see them before buying them

Freestanding: building that stands by itself, unattached to any other structure

Jewelry: necklaces, bracelets, rings, earrings

Matinees: morning and afternoon shows

Moustache: facial hair under the nose

No starch: don't put starch (a product that makes the material stiff) in the shirts

On the side: in a separate container, rather than mixed into the salad.

Pressed only: just ironed, not cleaned

Scan it: Scan the ticket at the register (The code may show a lower price.)

Sideburns: hair growing down a man's face in front of his ears

Store: keep at the cleaners until the next winter

Strip mall: a group of stores in a row with parking in front and back

To go: packaged to leave the restaurant so you don't eat the food there (You can eat take-out food at home, at your work, or in your car.)

Trim: a small amount of hair cut off to make one look neater

Utensils: knives, forks, spoons

Walk-ins: customers who walk in without appointments

Part 4 Notes Section

Appendix

Becoming an Active Learner in Your New Country

I f you are a reader, it is going to be easier to read in your native language. However, now you are reading for different reasons, not only for content, so you have to read in the target language, English. You are now reading for English vocabulary, **clues** from **context**, word similarity to words in your language, grammar, idioms, and slang. Therefore, read whatever you can **get your hands on**. Start simple and build up: read captions under pictures, headlines, and ads in newspapers that are too difficult to read in their **entirety** now. Read children's books, with or without children. All libraries have children's sections, and their librarians are very helpful. Additionally, there are interesting and informative yet easy ESL newspapers. One such paper is *Easy English News*. This paper contains news stories, information about U.S. culture, stories about holidays and events, letters from ESL students, idioms, **jokes**, **crossword puzzles** with answers, and vocabulary words defined. Check out the website, www.elizabethclaire.com, and click on "Easy English News."

When you are reading something, you may find words you do not understand. If there is time, **resist** the **urge** to pull out your automatic translator or bilingual dictionary. Use an English dictionary, but an easy one, which will define the word in English at your level. Getting the definition will take longer, but you will gain more vocabulary, perhaps see a drawing, and get a grammar explanation. McGraw-Hill offers many fine dictionaries of this type. Some may even have accompanying CDs so you may listen to the pronunciation of the words you are trying to define.

Always carry a small pad of paper and a pen or pencil with you in a pocket, a **purse** or **pocketbook**, or a **briefcase**. Write down anything you hear or read that you need to find out about later. You may hear unfamiliar idioms ("It's raining cats and dogs today") or slang ("I ate a **humongous** hamburger last night, so I don't want any lunch"). This writing is for your eyes only to **jog** your memory, so you don't have to make it perfect. Some of it can be in your native language.

Keep a journal in English. This can be in a larger notebook at home. **Set aside** a short time—at first, ten minutes—to write in your journal. Write in your journal every day, even if it is only a sentence or two to start. Write your thoughts about learning English, work, your new life, playing tennis. Write about your feelings, even if you have to write them in your own language, and look up the definitions for these feelings later.

Listen to the radio in the car, music **lyrics**, talk radio, the news. Watch TV, closed captioning, cartoons, and anything else. Even when you don't understand, listening to the sound of the language is helpful. Call a telephone number where you know nobody will answer (a movie theater, a business closed on weekends, a utility company, the weather, the time), and listen to the recorded message. Try to understand the **prompts**. Think about which voices are pleasing to you and which are not and why. Try to pattern your speech after the pleasant ones.

Books on CDs are other good avenues to try; you may listen to only a few minutes to see what you understand or get the book and read and listen at the same time. You may find a book that you have read in your language so that you are familiar with the setting, the characters, and the plot. **Immerse** yourself in English as much as you are able to. This does not mean you have to **deprive** yourself, or your children, of the joy of using your language; it means committing yourself to learning your new language as well and becoming truly bilingual.

Crossword puzzles are a great way to work on vocabulary. Don't start out with difficult ones; that could be **frustrating**. Try crossword puzzles for children or the ones in ESL books, magazines, or newspapers. There is much on the Internet, and a lot of it is very good and easily accessible. Check out *Dave's ESL Café*, www.eslcafe.com, and click on "Stuff for Students." This is only one of many sites, but an exciting one.

When speaking, always remember to speak English more slowly than you speak your own language. You will be surprised at the difference it makes in your **intelligibility**. Also, although you may be trying to hide your voice because you are **insecure** about your English, speak loudly and **project your voice**. If people can't hear you, you'll never really know if they could have understood you.

Idioms and Other Vocabulary

Briefcase: case with a handle used by businesspeople to carry papers

Clues: hints, information that helps you figure something out

Context: words that surround a word you are trying to figure out the meaning of (These words may help you to do so without having to look up the word.)

Crossword puzzles: forms in which you write the answers to questions or clues in a block pattern

Deprive: take something wanted away from someone

Entirety: complete form

Frustrating: making you feel upset because you cannot do what you want to do

Get your hands on: find

Handbag: *see* **Pocketbook**

Humongous: giant, very big

Immerse: put deep into

Insecure: without confidence in yourself

Intelligibility: ability to be understood

Jog: make you remember something

Jokes: funny stories that are supposed to make people laugh

Lyrics: words to music

Pocketbook (*also* **purse** *or* **handbag**): bag that ladies carry in which to put items they need, such as keys, money, cosmetics, and identification cards

Project your voice: speak so you are heard by everyone in a room

Prompts: what you hear when voice mail answers the telephone and tells you what to press or push to be connected

Purse: *see* **Pocketbook**

Resist: stop yourself

Set aside: plan for, schedule

Urge: strong desire or need to do something

About the Author

Natalie Gast (Hollywood, Florida) founded Customized Language Skills Training (CLST), a full-service language-training company in 1986. CLST provided tailor-made on-site training programs, including English as a Second Language (ESL), Accent Modification, Presentation Skills, and Writing Skills for the Foreign Born in business and industry. She also developed train-the-trainer programs for ESL instructors. Gast codeveloped "Supervising and Coaching Multicultural Workforces," cultural diversity materials and instructional sessions for several industries. She is the author of *Perfect Phrases for ESL: Everyday Business Life* and *Perfect Phrases for ESL: Advancing Your Career*. Gast earned her undergraduate degree at Boston University; her master's degree work in TESOL (Teaching English to Speakers of Other Languages) was done at Kean University, New Jersey. She moved from New Jersey to Hollywood, Florida, in 2010, where she consults in ESOL (English for Speakers of Other Languages), as it is called in Florida. Gast also conducts selected coaching and training programs.